Quilter, Granger, Grandma, Matriarch

Life on the Reiss Family Farm
1949-1953
St. Clair County, Illinois

Stephen W. Reiss

authorHOUSE®

AuthorHouse™
1663 Liberty Drive, Suite 200
Bloomington, IN 47403
www.authorhouse.com
Phone: 1-800-839-8640

First published by AuthorHouse 12/15/2008

ISBN: 978-1-4389-2756-5 (sc)
ISBN: 978-1-4389-2755-8 (hc)

Library of Congress Control Number: 2008910186

Printed in the United States of America
Bloomington, Indiana

This book is printed on acid-free paper.

Dedication

This book is dedicated to Catherine "Katie" Luetzelschwab Reiss because she wrote it, a day at a time over five years as her personal diary. Her love of family, neighbors, service, and rural life become evident to the reader as these days go by. Her character as matriarch to children, grandchildren, relatives, and friends is genuine because she lived her life never knowing that five years of it would be published. She was my grandmother, my dad's mom.

Acknowledgements

Several folks helped with elaborations (*in italics*) to make parts of Katie's diary a bit more self-explanatory. It was a combined effort of long-time neighbor Marcella Schilling Klein, nephew Lavern Lang, granddaughter June Ann Reiss McBrayer, and grand niece Gladys Hoffman Wittenauer. These folks knew Katie as a very special person and to an extent as a role model. They are all very special to me as well.

Stephen W. Reiss

The Stage and the Cast of Characters

Leading Lady: Catherine "Katie" Luetzelschwab was born on 3/25/1890 in St. Clair County, Illinois of Swiss parents. She had about six years of formal education and eventually worked as a domestic servant in the household of Frank and Anna Syvilla Reiss in 1910. There she met their oldest surviving son George Reiss and married him on 4/16/1911. Katie wrote the 5-year diary which appears below. It starts January 1949 when she is age 58 and her husband is age 75. She enjoyed quilting and volunteering at several area Grange halls, but never learned to drive an automobile. Her first language was German. Their three children were bi-lingual. Her diary is written in English.

Leading Man: George "Geo" or "Pop" Reiss was born on 4/22/1873 in St. Clair County, Illinois of German parents. He had about four years of formal education and worked for/with his parents on the family farm. He married his parents' domestic servant, Katie Luetzelschwab, on 4/16/1911. She was 17 years his junior. He and Katie eventually bought the family farm established by his grandfather Adam Reiss in 1834. George retired from farming in 1948 having farmed only with horses. He never owned a tractor. His vehicles were a 1925 Ford coupe and a 1930's pickup truck. His first language was German.

Supporting Cast One: Their first son is William "Bill" or "Willie" Reiss born 5/6/1912 on the family farm. He married Anita Hesse and had one surviving child, June Ann Reiss. They lived half an hour north in Maplewood, Illinois where he was a maintenance foreman with Socony Oil. They alternated visits for most Sunday evening meals with his Reiss parents and her Hesse parents who lived five miles apart.

Supporting Cast Two: Their second son is Franklin "Frank" Reiss born 10/31/1915 on the family farm. He married Gerry Hulet and had two sons, George Reiss and Richard Reiss. They lived two hours northeast in Urbana, Illinois where he was a professor of Agricultural Economics at the University of Illinois. They visited every three or four months.

Supporting Cast Three: Their third son is Irwin "Irv" Reiss born 9/18/1917 on the family farm. He married Mary Stephenson and had three children, Stephen "Steve" or "Stevie" Reiss, Kenneth "Ken" Reiss, and Mary Kay "Mickey" Reiss. They lived four hours east in Sullivan, Indiana where he was a professional farm manager with Meadowlark Farms which owned farm clusters near Denmark and Canton, both in Illinois, Chinook in Indiana, and other locations. They visited every three or four months. Irv often tied a visit home with a business visit to the Denmark farm which his mother often calls the "south" farm.

Other Cast – Her Relatives: Katie was the fifth of eleven Luetzelschwab children. Her sisters and their husbands who often visited were: Mary and Jacob Weihl, Minnie and John Sponemann, Lottie and Edward Sander, Lena and Joseph Speichinger, Caroline and Elmer Gummersheimer, and Edna and Henry Lang. Her brothers and their wives who often visited and occasionally helped with odd jobs were: Johnny and Katie, bachelor Herman, Jacob "Jaky" and Cora, and bachelor Frank. Other visitors were her married niece Elsie Weihl Hoffman and husband Albert.

Other Cast – His Relatives: George was the fourth of eleven Reiss children and the oldest of seven to reach adulthood. His sisters and their husbands who often visited were: Anna and George Dintelmann and widowed Katie Petry. His brothers and their wives who often visited were: John and Mary Etta from Sikeston, Henry and Bertha from St. Louis, Louis and Hattie from Texas, and Will and Rose from Belleville.

Other Cast – Neighbors: Katie and George could walk a quarter mile south to the farm of Frank and Clara Schilling or they could walk a quarter mile west to the farm of Ignatius "Boobie" and Marcella Klein. Marcella Klein is the Schilling's daughter which made the neighborhood even more friendly. "Boobie" is the German word for "boy" which was his childhood name that stuck. Katie and George had private telephone lines with those families that used old wooden wall-mounted crank telephones. They could also walk almost a mile west to the village of Floraville for church or meetings at the Floraville Grange. Other neighbors like the Metzgers, Koerbers, and Roushes often provided transportation help because Katie did not drive and George's vehicles were old and small. When Katie writes, for example, that Oscar Koerbers were here in the evening, she means both husband and wife.

Smithton Sportsmen's Club: This is a 40-acre parcel on the east edge of the Reiss Farm which Katie and George leased to this group of mostly fishermen in mid-1951. The Sportsmen built a clubhouse and put in three lakes which cover 11 acres. They have about 150 members and have been very supportive and partnering with the extended Reiss family for well over 50 years.

St. Paul United Church of Christ in Floraville: Katie and George were 50+ year members here. All three of their children were confirmed here. They attended regularly but were sometimes limited by weather and lack of transportation. Also in Floraville is a one-room brick school which all three of their sons attended.

Quilting and Patching: Katie found great relaxation and community in quilting. "Patching" is her word for making designs about a foot square which were then sewn together to create the overall quilt. Her diary below shows her quilting on 31 days in 1949, 58 days in 1950, 93 days in 1951, 61 days in 1952, and 43 days in 1953.

Grange Work: Katie found great satisfaction and accomplishment in volunteering at ten different Granges. She and George were founder members of the Floraville Grange from 3/8/1948. Her diary below shows her working at or working for various Granges on 31 days in 1949, 39 days in 1950, 29 days in 1951, 35 days in 1952, and 46 days in 1953. The National Grange was founded in 1867 in the aftermath of the Civil War. Peak national membership was 600,000. Illinois had 34 active Granges in 2008.

Farm Work: Katie's kitchen stove burned wood or corn cobs. In 1952 they upgraded to a new stove which was half electric and half solid fuel. One of George's major jobs was cutting firewood. They bought mail order baby chickens two or three times a year to raise and eventually sell meat and eggs in nearby communities. Those chicks started in the brooder house and were moved to a chicken house when old enough. A "brooder" is a sheet metal shelter about a foot tall and five feet in diameter with a central heat lamp which kept baby chicks warm. George and Katie also raised hogs and sold or butchered them as needed. They also received crop share income in renting out their farm after 1948. First tenant was the Howertons, second was the Josephs, and third was Lavern and Lucille Lang who started in April 1954. Lavern is Katie's nephew as the son of her sister Lena.

The Reiss Family Farm: Adam Reiss purchased 120 acres in 1834 for $1.25 per acre. Adjacent 40- and 20-acre parcels were purchased in 1854 and 1868, respectively, by Adam's widow Margaret and her second husband Conrad Ebert. Margaret's oldest son Frank Reiss and his wife Anne bought the 180-acre family farm from his mother and siblings in 1869. Their oldest son George Reiss and his wife Katie bought the family farm from his parents in 1920. George and Katie had previously bought 180 adjacent acres in 1917 from the Schaefer family. They continued to refer to those fields by the Schaefer name. The Reiss Family Farm continues to this day as 360 acres in Sections 7 and 8 of Prairie du Long Township in St. Clair County, Illinois.

Reiss Farm Buildings: Adam Reiss built a log cabin and a log barn in 1834. The cabin was home for his family of wife Margaret and five children. Then it was the home for his son Frank's family of wife Anne and ten children until 1889 when they built a modern six-room home nearby. The new house was then home for his son George's family of wife Katie and three sons until they built another modern seven-room home nearby in 1941. During these diary years, the two log buildings were used for farm storage. The farm tenants lived in the 1889 home and Katie and George lived in the 1941 home. The log barn continues to this day but sadly the log cabin was removed about 1975.

Katie's Diary

1949

January 1949

Sat 1 – Cloudy 22 degrees, warmed up to 35. We were in church. Henry was here when we came back. Fred Wachtels were here in evening. *Henry Lang is married to Katie's sister Edna. Their sons Lavern and Harold Lang are mentioned frequently below. The Langs have their own farm about 5 miles northwest. All three men were major helps to the Reisses.*

Sun 2 – Cloudy 32 warmed up to 45. We were at home all day. Gus and Alma came and took us along to Robert Probst's birthday party.

Mon 3 – Cloudy and foggy 45 degrees, 50 later and rain and thunder and lightning by evening. I worked on the Westerheide quilt.

Tues 4 – Rainy. Geo made firewood. I finished my quilt. In evening Geo and I were at Klein's.

Wed 5 – 27 degrees very stormy. In the evening we went to Elnora Kertis' for a Guild officers' meeting.

Thurs 6 – 30 degrees warmed up very nicely. I went to Clara to patch. She had a cold.

Fri 7 – 42 degrees in morning, warmed up to 60 by noon. We were at Millstadt at Guild meeting in evening.

Sat 8 – Cloudy still warm. I did my Saturday work. Geo worked by the branch.

Sun 9 – Cloudy. We went to the church meeting in afternoon. In evening Jack and Virginia were here to get the quilt.

Mon 10 – 45 degrees rained all night and was rainy all day. Mrs. Westerheide was here.

Tues 11 – 36 degrees foggy and misty all day. I helped butcher at Schilling's and we took our two hogs to Schilling's in the evening to butcher tomorrow.

Wed 12 – 33 degrees cloudy, drizzling. I helped Schillings butcher our two hogs. Geo helped too, but went home to do the feeding at noon. *Frank and Clara Schilling lived half a mile south through the woods. He was also a beekeeper. Their two sons often helped the Reisses with projects.*

Thurs 13 – 32 degrees cloudy, getting warm. We had officers' installation at our Grange. Beulah did the installing. I acted as marshal. We had lunch.

Fri 14 – Cloudy warmer 40 degrees. I went with Schilling's to file income report at Broad Hollow Grange.

Sat 15 – Partly cloudy warm 52 degrees. I did my Saturday work. Geo had some wheat crushed at Frank Klein's.

Sun 16 – Rainy all day colder. Uncle Will was here. In the evening at 8 o'clock, Mary & Irwin and children came to stay over the week. *Will Reiss is George's youngest brother who is married to Rose. He had no children and was "uncle" to everyone. They live in Belleville.*

Mon 17 – Colder light snow didn't get above 22 all day. Irwin went to the stockyards. We stayed home. Willie, Anita & June came for supper. *Willie is their oldest son and lives in Maplewood.*

Tues 18 – Rain all day freezing to a solid ice, trees and telephone wires down. Couldn't hardly walk outside.

Wed 19 – 20 above. Mary, Irwin and Stevie went to Columbia, Mo. and stayed till Thursday night. Geo and I kept Ken and Mary Kay. *Irwin is their youngest son and lives in Sullivan, Indiana.*

Thurs 20 – 11 above fair. Franklin came in the evening at 5:30. Mary & Irwin & Stevie got home at around seven o'clock. *Franklin is their middle son and lives in Urbana, Illinois.*

Fri 21 – 25 above. Irwin, Mary & Pop were at Waterloo Bank. Franklin & I went to Belleville afternoon. Bill, Anita & June came in evening.

Sat 22 – 30 degrees. Franklin left for home in the morning and Irwin & Mary left after dinner for home. Cloudy & thawing some.

Sun 23 – Rain all day, very foggy. We were at church. Consistory members were installed. Oscar Koerbers were here in evening.

Mon 24 – Rain all day, colder by night freezing ice. We couldn't do much work of any kind.

Tues 25 – Misty, freezing ice. I went to Clara's and helped quilt. It was slick to walk, 26 degrees all day.

Wed 26 – Rainy all day, freezing slick ice on everything, 28 degrees. Franklin and Geo came in evening. Franklin went to Sparta meeting, got back at 11 o'clock evening.

Thurs 27 – 30 degrees rain all day foggy. Franklin and Georgie left for home at 9:30. I patched and ironed. Geo did the feeding.

Fri 28 – Partly cloudy colder. I sewed all day. Geo made firewood. Frank Klein & Charlie were here to make plans for sale.

Sat 29 – Cold, zero. I sewed some more and did my Saturday work. Baked bread & coffee cake.

Sun 30 – Cold 2 above zero, very little snow on the ground. Henry Langs and Boobie Kleins all were here in afternoon. *The Kleins live a quarter mile west.*

Mon 31 – 10 above. I worked about the house. Geo did the feeding.

February 1949

Tues 1 – Fair 17 degrees but warmed up to 35 & 40. We went to Millstadt in the truck.

Wed 2 – Fair very pretty day but turning cloudy by night. I washed afternoon. I was at the church quilting in evening. I ironed everything.

Thurs 3 – 33 degrees, some snow sleet then turned to an all day rain. We got the hamburger meat at Knab's for the sale.

Fri 4 – Cloudy 30 degrees. I baked coffee cake and patched. Geo did the feeding and made firewood.

Sat 5 – Cloudy 33 degrees. We were at the Stratton sale to serve refreshments. In evening Gus and Alma were here.

Sun 6 – Cloudy to showers at times. Frank & Lena Klein brought my pots and pans home from the sale. We cleared $157.60.

Mon 7 – Fair 20 degrees in morning, warmed up to 42 by noon. Geo & I cut brush by road along Klein's here.

Tues 8 – Fair warmer. I went quilting at church hall with Alma & Gus. It got colder in evening. We cleaned brush along road.

Wed 9 – 24 degrees fair getting warmer. Clara was here in afternoon. In morning Geo and I cleaned up brush along the branch.

Thurs 10 – 28 degrees very stormy from NW. We stayed in the house mostly all day. Went to Grange meeting in evening.

Fri 11 – 28 degrees but warmed up a lot during the day, strong south wind all day. Joe Roths were here in evening.

Sat 12 – 44 degrees partly cloudy strong south winds. I baked bread & coffee cake & did my Saturday work. Geo made firewood.

Sun 13 – Cloudy all day, rain by night. We were home all day.

Mon 14 – Rain and icy all day. Thunder & lightning by afternoon & night, hard rains, warmer. We quilted at Marcella's.

Tues 15 – Fair cooler. Had a large crowd at our card party.

Wed 16 – Fair 36 degrees cloudy. Alma and I were to the quilting at the church hall.

Thurs 17 – Fair, we worked about the place.

Fri 18 – Fair, we cleaned the brooder house and set up the brooder and put some straw into it.

Sat 19 – Fair very pretty day warm. I baked and did my Saturday work.

Sun 20 – Cloudy to fair, no frost. I was at church, then Bill, Anita and June Ann came for dinner. In evening we were to Marcella's birthday party.

Mon 21 – Cloudy light rains. We took 2 hogs to Streck's, 445 lbs @ $21.35. Afternoon I worked in the house. Geo made firewood.

Tues 22 – Cold northwest wind cloudy. I had a cold so I stayed in the house and cut quilt patches & sewed a slip and handkerchiefs.

Wed 23 – Cloudy no frost. Clara and I went to Fred Wachtel's quilting. Geo sowed red clover on Crooks' land then he came to Wachtel's in evening.

Thurs 24 – Cloudy to fair, light rain colder. We build hog shed for the red hogs. In evening Metzgers took us along to Broad Hollow Grange card party.

Fri 25 – Fair 22 in morning, 50 by noon. I sewed in morning. Afternoon I helped Clara patch. Geo mixed feed.

Sat 26 – Fair. I sewed and Geo worked about outside.

Sun 27 – Cloudy cold east wind, rained & snowed some. We stayed home all day. It was Sunday.

Mon 28 – Cold stormy, fair. I sewed quilt patches. Geo did the feeding.

March 1949

Tues 1 – Cold windy around 20, sunshiney. I went quilting at Ethel Vogle's afternoon and evening.

Wed 2 – Fair cold. We worked about the place and I sewed some.

Thurs 3 – Fair getting warmer. We took hens & eggs to Millstadt. Then Clara & I went quilting to Anna Wachtel's.

Fri 4 – Fair very pretty day no frost. I raked in the yard. Henry Lang brought some fish for our pond.

Sat 5 – Fair very warm 73 by afternoon. We worked about the place. Sowed some lettuce. Thundershower by night.

Sun 6 – Fair cold wind all day. Henry & Bertha, Bill & Anita & June were here during the day. Elsie & Art Chattillion came in evening. *Henry Reiss is George's younger brother. He is a pharmacist in St. Louis.*

Mon 7 – Partly cloudy 24 in morning. We tore off the coal shed and made a brooder house shed of it.

Tues 8 – 44 degrees partly cloudy. We got our 300 two week old chicks today. We were at the Woodman card party. I won a broom, Pop a waste basket.

Wed 9 – Rainy all day. I went to Belleville with Schillings to make out income tax. Started to snow at 8 in evening and electric went off at 8:30.

Thurs 10 – 28 degrees still without electric but it came on at 3:00 PM. Then we moved our chicks out again. Snow is 4 to 5 inches deep and drifted badly.

Fri 11 – 26 degrees fair. We dug our way out so we could go to Millstadt to pay our income tax $168.00. Got $.39 for eggs today. Starter feed $5.20.

Sat 12 – 24 degrees fair snow melted quite a bit. I sewed and Pop cut some firewood.

Sun 13 – 28 degrees. 3 inch snow fell in the night. Now it's partly cloudy to four. We were at Schilling's in the afternoon.

Mon 14 – Fair to cloudy & colder. Boobie took us along to the telephone meeting in evening. I also called up Irwin & Mary, then I quilted at church hall.

Tues 15 – 17 above in morning, fair to warmer, snow melted a lot. I sewed all day. Geo cut firewood.

Wed 16 – Cloudy all day 24 degrees. We got up early and took Verna to Millstadt, also took our eggs along. Got $.39 a doz and $.34/lb for hens.

Thurs 17 – 40 degrees, fair to cloudy, rain sleet thundering by afternoon and snow, muddy. Stahls brought the load of red clover hay. I sewed quilt patches. Geo couldn't do anything but the feeding.

Fri 18 – Fair 22 degrees, last night snow melted again, about 3 inches had fallen with sleet & rain also lightninged & thundered while it snowed in the evening.

Sat 19 – 30 degrees. Fair to cloudy, some snow by afternoon, again fair in evening around 35 degrees. Ground is awful wet.

Sun 20 – No frost fair windy. The birthday club came in the evening to celebrate my birthday. 23 were here.

Mon 21 – Cloudy warm 60 degrees very stormy from the south rain by late afternoon. Pop & I were at my Home Bureau meeting at Ed Groth's.

Tues 22 – Cloudy NW winds 46 degrees. Ground is very wet. I worked about the house. Geo couldn't do much.

Wed 23 – Fair getting warmer. We worked about the place.

Thurs 24 – Fair getting warmer. We worked about the place. I got a lot of birthday cards. Were at Grange meeting in evening.

Fri 25 – Fair warm, the prettiest day we had for a long time. I washed and helped Geo saw up some trees. Irwin called in evening.

Sat 26 – Fair to rain. I did my Saturday work and prepared for Sunday company.

Sun 27 – Fair but very stormy cold. Ralph & Viola and family, Katy Petry, Henry & Bertha, Bill, Anita & June all were here for dinner. We were at Marie Koerber's birthday in the evening. *Katy Petry is George's widowed younger sister. Viola Bald is her married daughter.*

Mon 28 – Fair warm very pretty day. We butchered a hog and worked about the place.

Tues 29 – Fair very warm to cloudy, hard rain in the night. We took meat to the locker. Got $.39 for eggs. Paid $5.20 for chick starter.

Wed 30 – Light rain during the day. Irwin was at the cattle sale at Belleville and then came home to spend the night with us.

Thurs 31 – Cloudy strong NW winds cold 45. Irwin left this morning. Then I sewed & patched. Geo made firewood.

April 1949

Fri 1 – Very cloudy, cold 43. We took 2 hogs to Belleville. Afternoon Mr. & Mrs. Gerhold were here. I worked about the yard.

Sat 2 – Very cloudy, 42 degrees. We took out the brooder as chicks are 5 ½ weeks old and all feathered. We cleaned the brooder house.

Sun 3 – 40 degrees rainy all morning, clearing afternoon. We were at church then had consistory meeting. Schillings were here in evening.

Mon 4 – 42 degrees fair. We worked about the place cleaning up the old brooder house.

Tues 5 – Cloudy to fair and again cloudy with light showers by evening. We went voting and then to Millstadt to get chick feed.

Wed 6 – Very pretty day 50 to 60 degrees. We tore down part of the old brooder house. Were at church in evening. Trimmed pigs today.

Thurs 7 – Fair to a few light showers. I worked about the yard all day. Left our chicks out in the yard today.

Fri 8 – Fair very pretty day 46 to 58 degrees, northwest wind. We took 3 red hogs to Streck's. I also planted cannas & baked cookies & a cake.

Sat 9 – Fair to cloudy. Cool 50 degrees. Franklin, Gerry, and the boys came at noon. Bill and June came afternoon. Anita was at the school elections at Maple Wood.

Sun 10 – Very cloudy & rainy in morning cold around 48 to 50. After dinner Franklin took some pictures of the Floraville Grange. Bill, Anita & June were here in evening.

Mon 11 -- Cloudy, getting a bit warmer. Franklin, Gerry, and the boys left for home this morning. We got 25 bu oats at Ed Groth's. Then we worked about the place. Geo was at the telephone meeting in evening.

Tues 12 – Fair very pretty day. We got a load of oats at Ed Groth's. Afternoon I worked in the garden. Planted cannas. Geo cleared the telephone line.

Wed 13 – Fair very warm 75 degrees. Patsy & I were at the Home Bureau play day at Progressive Grange. Early in morning Geo & I got oats at Ed Groth's.

Thurs 14 – A thunder shower in early morning, 65 in morning, 45 at night. We went to Millstadt at 10:30 a.m. and it thundered & rained hard there. Today was Holy Thursday. Very strong west winds.

Fri 15 – 36 degrees, partly cloudy, cold strong NW winds a little sprinkle afternoon. Today is Good Friday. We could not go to church as I had a cold.

Sat 16 – Still strong NW winds, 32 degrees ground frozen and ice on water. Fair warmed up to 50 by noon. Geo had some wheat ground. I did my Saturday work. Mrs. Roush and son were here a while.

Sun 17 – Easter Sunday. Fair cold winds. We were at church, then had consistory right after church. In evening we went to Turkey Hill Grange with Metzgers.

Mon 18 – Fair still cold no frost tho. Home Bureau meeting at Mrs. Elsie Etling's. We went to Belleville, then to Freeburg and in the evening the Birthday Club came for Pop's birthday.

Tues 19 – Frost fair warmer. We went to Ed Groth's to get the last oats. Then I washed and worked in the garden.

Wed 20 – Light frost, fair. I worked in the garden all day. Lorena Skaer came and got plants. I planted beans today also cannas & dahlias.

Thurs 21 – Fair warmer. We went to Millstadt got my hair fixed. Afternoon I did more spading and planting.

Fri 22 – Fair warmer a very pretty day. Will & Lena Feder were here. We worked about the place. I went along with Bill & Anita to their home in evening. *Will Feder is a cousin to George since his mother's maiden name was Feder.*

Sat 23 – Fair very pretty day. We left at Bill & Anita's at 8 o'clock to go to Mary & Irwin's. Got there by 12:30 had a very enjoyable trip.

Sun 24 – Fair warm. We had a lovely visit with Mary & Irv and the children. Went to see the park and left for home by 3 o'clock.

Mon 25 – Fair cooler. We were at the play at our Grange last night. Today we worked about the place.

Tues 26 – Fair. Irwin, Mary, and the children came towards evening. Irwin left for Kansas in evening. Mary & children stayed here. Pop & I went to Grange.

Wed 27 – No entry.

Thurs 28 – No entry.

Fri 29 – Fair to cloudy cool. Emma Barthel and her daughters were here to get flowers. Then we all walked to Klein's for awhile.

Sat 30 – Fair cool. Irwin came back from his trip. Then they went to Belleville to get things. In evening they went to dinner & dance with Bill & Anita.

May 1949

Sun 1 – Fair hot. Bill & Anita and June were here, we all had dinner together then Irwin, Mary & children left for home. Got a heavy shower by 4 o'clock.

Mon 2 – Fair. We worked about the place. Started to clean the hen house.

Tues 3 – Fair hot. I worked in the yard & garden. Geo shucked corn and did some grinding.

Wed 4 – Fair hot 90 degrees. We started work on the chicken summer house. We also were at Millstadt with the eggs.

Thurs 5 – Very hot 95, hottest May day we ever had. We worked on the summer house in morning & afternoon Mrs. Westerheide & Mrs. Roush were here. Geo was to the Jim Miller funeral.

Fri 6 – Fair hot 90 degrees. We worked on the chicken yard fence. Afternoon I washed. Boobie came in evening and fixed our telephone line. Shower in night.

Sat 7 – Much cooler. We fixed the yard by the summer house and moved the chickens in. John & Audry came in the morning. *John Reiss is George's younger brother. He owns the Reiss Dairy in Sikeston, Missouri. Audry is his daughter.*

Sun 8 – Cool fair to cloudy, light drizzle early in morning and thundershowers by evening. We were at Edna's for dinner. Bill & Anita and June came towards eve.

Mon 9 – Cloudy cool thundershower by afternoon, also some rain during the night. Geo & I were at the telephone meeting at Floraville in evening.

Tues 10 – Fair cool 56 degrees. We got 250 baby chicks today. We also cleaned the old hen house and sprayed it.

Wed 11 – Very cool 42 degrees. Planted watermelons & beans. Shucked some corn.

Thurs 12 – Fair. We celebrated Mothers Day at the Grange. I had to give the program. We had a nice time and good eats.

Fri 13 – Fair hot. I painted the coupe after we came back from Smithton.

Sat 14 – Fair, getting hot. I waxed the coupe and cleaned out the shed for it and did my Saturday work.

Sun 15 – Fair to partly cloudy. We were at church, then we visited with John Rapps. Roushes were here in evening.

Mon 16 – Fair. We were at my Home Bureau meeting at the house of Mrs. Clarence Herman.

Tues 17 – Cool in morning, 86 by noon, fair. We shucked some corn today then I baked coffee cake. Mrs. Monroe Probst died today.

Wed 18 – Cloudy cool. I picked 5 boxes strawberries then helped Geo shuck corn. Hot by afternoon. Then I worked about the place.

Thurs 19 – Heavy rain in morning. We took our eggs and 10 springers (*chickens*) to Millstadt, $.39 for eggs, $.32 for springers. We also went to see Irma Probst.

Fri 20 – Cloudy cool. We shucked a load of corn, then we went to Irma Probst's funeral.

Sat 21 – Heavy rain in morning, afternoon we went Elsie Hesse's shower at Seibert's. In the evening it rained again.

Sun 22 – Misty cold in morning, fair in afternoon. We had our strawberries at the Grange in Floraville. Lottie & Ed were here in afternoon.

Mon 23 – Fair. I helped clean the hall then I washed it. Pop worked about the place.

Tues 24 – Fair. We shucked corn and I picked my last strawberries.

Wed 25 – Fair cool. We shucked corn and I worked in the yard.

Thurs 26 – Fair cool 58 degrees. I was at Belleville with Boobie and Marcella. We were to our Grange meeting in the evening.

Fri 27 – Light drizzle to fair very cool 57 degrees. We took 39 spring chickens to Vernon Albert's, got 32 cents a lb. We worked about the place.

Sat 28 – Fair. We shucked 3 rows of corn then I did my Saturday work.

Sun 29 – Fair to cloudy cool. Herman & Frank were here.

Mon 30 – Fair. We cleaned the hen house and the brooder house and took the brooder out. Chicks are three weeks old now.

Tues 31 – Fair. We shucked a load of corn, then I went to our spring festival at our church. Women from 4 other churches were here.

June 1949

Wed 1 – Cloudy heavy rain in early morning. Afternoon I went to Waterloo church with Ida Gasser. In evening to Paul Wachtel's wedding dance.

Thurs 2 – Fair to cloudy, cool all day. Mrs. Roush and I visited with Mrs. Westerheide all day.

Fri 3 – Fair, hot 88 degrees by noon. We were at Millstadt & Belleville to get feed. Afternoon I worked in the garden.

Sat 4 – 73 degrees in early morning, fair. We gathered corn in the morning. Afternoon I worked about the place.

Sun 5 – Fair not so hot, very pretty day. Mr. & Mrs. Stephenson came around 3 o'clock afternoon. We all went to Elsie Hesse's wedding.

Mon 6 – Rained quite a bit. I worked in the house. Mr. & Mrs. Stephenson left for Indiana in the morning. *Andrew and Daisy Stephenson are the parents of Irwin Reiss' wife, Mary. They live in California and drove from there to visit with Mary and family in Sullivan, Indiana.*

Tues 7 – Fair. We gathered corn and then I worked in the garden.

Wed 8 – Getting hot, but cloudy all day so I worked in my strawberry plants.

Thurs 9 – Fair hot. We gathered corn in morning. Afternoon I was at Clara's to help patch. Grange meeting in evening. Rain in night.

Fri 10 – We picked 2 gallons of dewberries, I canned 7 quarts. Hard shower by night.

Sat 11 – We gathered corn and also picked 2 ½ gal dewberries, canned 6 quarts. We were at Geo Hendrick's and paid the oats, $98.60.

Sun 12 – We picked some berries. Uncle Will came in the afternoon.

Mon 13 – We husked corn & picked berries. I canned some. I cleaned in the chicken house.

Tues 14 – We husked corn and picked berries. We had an awful hard rain by evening and in the night.

Wed 15 – We husked corn and then I worked about the place. Geo mixed feed. Picked 2 gal berries for Marcella and canned 12 quarts of cherries which Clara picked.

Thurs 16 – We husked 3 rows of corn. I planted some butter beans and weeded the garden.

Fri 17 – We husked 3 rows of corn and picked berries and I worked about the house & yard. We took eggs to Millstadt & got feed.

Sat 18 – We husked 3 rows of corn and picked some berries. Roushes and Bill & Anita were here towards evening to get chickens.

Sun 19 – Fair hot. We picked some berries, a lot of berries were picked by other people. Henry & Edna and family were here in evening. *Edna Lang is Katie's youngest sister.*

Mon 20 – Fair hot. We were to the Home Bureau meeting at Mrs. Frank Joseph's. Also had some feed ground.

Tues 21 – Fair after a heavy shower early in morning. We picked some dewberries. Seiberts also came and picked. Schillings started to combine the hard wheat today.

Wed 22 – Fair hot 88 degrees. Schillings combined wheat in the sheep pasture. Apricots are ripe.

Thurs 23 – Fair hot around 90. Schillings finished in sheep pasture. We picked 3 gal dewberries and also some apricots.

Fri 24 – Fair. Henry Lang started to combine in the Schaefer ground. We picked dewberries. I canned 14 pints. *The Schaefer ground is 180 adjoining acres George and Katie bought in 1917 from the Schaefers.*

Sat 25 – Fair hot over 90 by noon. I picked dewberries for ourselves and did my Saturday work. *Dewberries are a cousin to blackberries but grow on wild vines only a foot tall. Requires a lot of bending over to pick.*

Sun 26 – Thunderstorm, heavy rain in morning. Henry, Berta, Will, and Bill & Anita & June were here.

Mon 27 – Fair hot 95 by afternoon. I picked 2 gal cherries. Bill, Anita & June took 2 gals cherries along last night.

Tues 28 – Hot. I picked 3 gal cherries. They are all now. Pop brought in more apricots. These late cherries should not be picked later than June 20th. They are over ripe now & rot.

Wed 29 – Very hot. Henry Lang finished combining this morning. By one o'clock we had a heavy rain, still very hot 95 now.

Thurs 30 – Very hot 99 by afternoon. Mary & Irwin left for Montana at noon today. The children are here with us. *Several of the farm clusters which Irwin managed for Meadowlark Farms raised sheep. This trip to Montana was for buying sheep.*

July 1949

Fri 1 – 85 degrees at 8 o'clock a.m., fair. I had my work with the children. Pop mixed feed. We mailed 3 dollars to the Successful Farmers paper for renewal for 3 years.

Sat 2 – Fair hot. I couldn't do more than take care of the children.

Sun 3 – Fair hot. Bill, Anita and June came in the evening. They brought fireworks. June stayed here for the week.

Mon 4 – Fair hot. We did only our cooking and cared for the children. Irwin called up in the evening from Montana.

Tues 5 – Fair hot. We washed and ironed. Taxes for 1948 were $280.31 for our land and everything.

Wed 6 – Fair hot. We canned apple sauce and took care of the children.

Thurs 7 – Partly cloudy, hot. I washed and peeled apples. By five o'clock we got the hardest rain ever. Creeks were out.

Fri 8 – Hot. We baked cookies and washed and picked blackberries, and took care of the children.

Sat 9 – Fair. June Ann & I canned apple sauce and made jelly. Bill & Anita came and took June along home.

Sun 10 – Fair cooler. Mary & Irv came back from their trip to Montana. We all went to the Turner picnic in the evening.

Mon 11 – Fair warm. We all went to the Meadowlark Farms today. *This visit to Meadowlark Farms refers to the farm cluster near Denmark, Illinois about 60 miles south.*

Tues 12 – Fair cool, hot by noon. Mary & I canned apple sauce and Bill, Anita & June came in the evening.

Wed 13 – Cool, cloudy all day. Mary & Irv and children left for Indiana today. I picked berries and made jelly.

Thurs 14 – 68 degrees, fair to hot, NW winds. We took wheat to Millstadt, got $1.69 a bu, test 57. Afternoon I worked in the flowers. Our 1948 papers were signed for payment today.

Fri 15 – Cloudy. We took the last of Crooks third wheat to Belleville today. Then we stopped at Edna's. Had a shower by evening. Mr. Louis rented the wheat land today.

Sat 16 – Partly cloudy cool only 80 degrees at noon. I'm doing my Saturday work. Geo is gathering corn.

Sun 17 – Fair cooler. We were at Elmer & Carolina's today. Katie Petry was here as we came home and she will stay here this week. *Carolina Gummersheimer is Katie's younger sister.*

Mon 18 – Partly cloudy, light shower and cooler. Patsy came and we went to the Home Bureau meeting at the home of Lucille Koch.

Tues 19 – Cloudy heavy rain, creeks were out. We canned apple sauce. We picked 4 gal blackberries for Roy Moskopf. We paid our taxes today $280.31.

Wed 20 – Partly cloudy. We patched all day. Getting hot again. I washed by hand what was dirty since Sunday.

Thurs 21 – Showers. We picked up more apples and canned some. Also ironed. We paid the Millstadt taxes today.

Fri 22 – Rained a good shower. I washed some things again, very hot and sultry. Temperature around 95 every day.

Sat 23 – Fair hot. We dressed chickens and prepared things for Sunday dinner. Went to the Paderborn picnic towards evening.

Sun 24 – Partly cloudy some cooler. Ralph & Viola came for dinner and afternoon we all went to Bill & Anita's, also to their picnic. *Viola Bald is George's niece.*

Mon 25 – Hot 97 degrees, showers all morning. I washed. Clearing by afternoon. Boobie and Marcella took us along to the Fair at Belleville.

Tues 26 – Fair, hot 95 degrees. I worked about the house. Irwin called from Freeburg. He came through on an inspection trip.

Wed 27 – Fair very hot. I was at Clara's a little while in the afternoon. We worked about the place.

Thurs 28 – We were at the Belleville Fair today. Hot.

Fri 29 – Hot.

Sat 30 – Hot.

Sun 31 – Fair cool. We were at church, then Rapps came. In evening we went to the Smithton picnic with Metzgers.

August 1949

Mon 1 – Cool 60 degrees. Franklin, Gerry and the boys came in the afternoon. Rained hard at night.

Tues 2 – Fair cool. Were at John & Katie's for dinner, then stopped at Edna & Henry's. Kleins & Schillings were here in evening. *John Luetzelschwab is Katie's brother. Edna Lang is her sister.*

Wed 3 – Fair cool all day. We were at Uncle Henry & Aunt Bertha's for dinner, then to the zoo. Had supper at Bill & Anita's. *Henry Reiss is George's brother and lives in St. Louis.*

Thurs 4 – Fair. We were at Chester Seibert's for supper.

Fri 5 – Fair getting hot again. We were at Carlina's, Melva's, Pearl's and Sister Mary's and Lottie & Ed. Franklin & Gerry opera in evening. *Carlina (actually Caroline) Gummersheimer, Mary Weihl, and Lottie Sander are Katie's sisters. Melva Gummersheimer and Pearl Schuchardt are her nieces.*

Sat 6 – Fair quite hot. Franklin got some package for us. Afternoon they went to Emile Hendrich's for supper.

Sun 7 – Fair. We left early for Sikeston. Got there at eleven o'clock had a nice visit and dinner at Lonnie & Lillian's. *Lillian Reiss Standley is the married daughter of George's brother John Reiss in Sikeston, Missouri. John and son-in-law Lonnie Standley own the Reiss Dairy there.*

Mon 8 – Cloudy. We came back from our Mo. trip this evening. It's getting hotter again.

Tues 9 – Today we stayed home and rested.

Wed 10 – Franklin & Gerry the boys and I all went to Granite City and Horse Shoe Lake to take pictures.

Thurs 11 – Hot, thundershower. Franklin and family left for home today. I worked about the house.

Fri 12 – Rained hard early then cloudy all day. We were at Belleville. Kenneth & Evelyn Bevirt and Emily Reiss were here. *Evelyn Bevirt and Emily Reiss are George's nieces.*

Sat 13 – Fair very hot. I washed all the bed things and picked and canned some peaches. Around 95 degrees.

Sun 14 – Fair very warm sultry 95 degrees. We were at church and consistory meeting. Jack Westerheides were here in afternoon, in evening Clara's birthday.

Mon 15 – Cloudy, rained & shower by afternoon. We were at Mrs. Hesse's Home Bureau meeting.

Tues 16 – Fair not quite so hot. I helped cook at Eileen Klein's wedding. Boobie and Marcella took us to the dance in evening.

Wed 17 – Hot today around 95. We took some hens to Millstadt got 20 cents a lb. Afternoon we rested.

Thurs 18 – Hot around 95. I worked about the house also pulled some weeds and picked the last of the Belle of Georgia peaches.

Fri 19 – Partly cloudy very hot, had a bad storm by four o'clock, rained hard. Took roof off our summer house. I ironed.

Sat 20 – Much cooler, 62 in morning, cool all day. I mowed the lawn. We put the roof back on again and put up the new metal nests.

Sun 21 – Fair 62, cool all day. I helped cook at the Hecker picnic.

Mon 22 – Fair cool 62 in morning. Had quite a bit of company during the day. Henry Lang came to mow wheat land.

Tues 23 – Fair cool 62 in morning. We took 2 hogs to Streck's. Mary Klein & Mrs. Roush were here afternoon. *Streck's is a butcher shop in Belleville who would buy hogs and/or do custom butchering.*

Wed 24 – Fair 65 degrees in morning. We chopped trees & brush along the road. In evening Rollie, Barbara, Nancy, Carl, Katie & Mueths were here. *Rollie Luetzelschwab is Katie's nephew with wife and three children. The Mueths are neighbors.*

Thurs 25 – Fair getting hotter. We cut trees & brush along the road. Then went to Millstadt, got hit by a car.

Fri 26 – Fair, hot. We were at Belleville to report on car accident. Mrs. Roush was here afternoon.

Sat 27 – Rain by noon. I cleaned the porch and put up drapes in living room.

Sun 28 – Light rain in early morning, then fair & cooler. I baked 2 cakes and dressed a chicken.

Mon 29 – Fair cool. We had a committee meeting at church hall. Planned to have a picnic on the 2nd of October.

Tues 30 – Fair cool. I cleaned the house and sun porch and prepared for company. Dressed 3 chickens.

Wed 31 – Louis & Hattie were here all day & night. We all went to Bill & Anita's for supper. It was very cold around 54 by morning. *Louis Reiss is George's brother. They live in Texas where he is a refrigeration engineer.*

September 1949

Thurs 1 – Fair cool 54 degrees. I baked rolls & coffee cake. Irwin, Mary & children came in the afternoon. Rained a lot.

Fri 2 – Fair very cool 44 degrees. We didn't do much but just visited together. Irwin was at the Illinois Farm till evening.

Sat 3 – Fair. Irwin, Mary, Ken & Stevie and June Ann went to the zoo. In the evening, Louis & Hattie and the McCalls and Bill & Anita were here. *The married daughter of Louis & Hattie Reiss is Syvilla McCall who lives with her family in Centralia, Illinois.*

Sun 4 – Fair to cloudy rain by night. We all went to the Millstadt homecoming for awhile.

Mon 5 – Fair. Henry and Brinkers were here. In evening I went to church committee meeting also Home Ec meeting. We worked on our scrap book.

Tues 6 – Fair cool. Irwin & Mary and the children left for home this morning, and Geo & I took two hogs to Streck's, 215 and 265 lbs.

Wed 7 – Cloudy to fair. I was at Mueth's all day to cook for the wedding. Boobie & Marcella took us to the reception in the evening.

Thurs 8 – Fair cooler. Sister Mary and Lillian were here all day. We were at the Grange meeting in the evening. *Mary Weihl is Katie's widowed sister. Lillian is her daughter.*

Fri 9 – Fair 50 degrees. We took 2 hogs to Streck's. They only weighed 350 lbs together. Afternoon I was at Schilling's awhile.

Sat 10 – Fair cool 48 degrees. I washed a very big wash. Geo helped C. Louis spread fertilizer on Schaefer's place.

Sun 11 – Cloudy all day, rain by night. We were at church, then afternoon we were at Broad Hollow Grange chicken supper. Also visited Roushes awhile.

Mon 12 – Thundershowers all day, rained very hard at times. I worked on the scrapbook and finished up some hickory nuts.

Tues 13 – Fair cool. Patsy Glauber and I were at Daab's Clubhouse to the Home Bureau meeting. Pot luck dinner.

Wed 14 – Cloudy plenty rain by night. We went to A. Barthel's and went to Woodland Grange Pomona meeting with them.

Thurs 15 – I worked about the house. Geo mixed feed. Rained hard last night.

Fri 16 – Cloudy cool. We took some old hens to Millstadt, got 19 cents a lb, eggs 50 a doz. We moved some chickens in the winter house.

Sat 17 – Cloudy all day, warmer. I moved some chickens and did my Saturday work. Geo husked corn and mixed feed.

Sun 18 – Fair warm, rained during the night. We were at the Grange outing. Bill, Anita and June Ann were here in the evening.

Mon 19 – I made a mistake, this is for the 20th of Sept. 56 degrees fair. We took hens to Smithton, 21 cents/lb. Had the truck steering fixed. Then we worked on the road a bit.

Tues 20 – This is for the 19th. Fair cool. We worked around the place. In the evening we were at Prosperity Grange with Barthels.

Wed 21 – Fair cool 57 degrees. We worked about the place.

Thurs 22 – Fair cold 58 degrees. We were to the Grange meeting. Potted some plants.

Fri 23 – We worked about the house and place. Potted more plants.

Sat 24 – Fair. I did my Saturday work and baked a cake.

Sun 25 – Fair. We were at church stayed home afternoon. In evening were at Frank Schilling's birthday party.

Mon 26 – Fair. I worked with the chickens and yard.

Tues 27 – Fair cold. We worked about the place.

Wed 28 – I moved the young chickens so we can clean the brooder house. Cold NW winds.

Thurs 29 – We worked hard to prepare for our chicken dinner Sunday, also picked some apples. Cleaned the brooder house. Cold NW winds.

Fri 30 – Fair very pretty day. Mary & Irv & family came afternoon. In evening Irv took us to the Booster night at our Grange. Frost 35 degrees.

October 1949

Sat 1 – Fair warm & windy. We butchered 59 chickens at the hall for the dinner tomorrow. Irwin & Bill were at the Farms. *This is the cluster farm near Denmark, Illinois.*

Sun 2 – Cloudy showery. We had our church chicken dinner, started at 12 noon till about 7 in the evening.

Mon 3 – Cloudy all day, rains by night. Irwin & Mary left for Texas this morning. I took care of the children.

Tues 4 – Rain all day. I baked and took care of the children. Irwin called from Texas in the evening.

Wed 5 – Rainy all day, warm. I just took care of the children and butchered chickens. Douglas Roush fixed our kitchen light.

Thurs 6 – Cloudy to fair. Mrs. Roush and sons were here in evening. Douglas fixed our kitchen light switch. Not yesterday.

Fri 7 – Fair very warm and windy. Geo made cider. I baked rolls & bread and cleaned around here. Mary & Irwin came back in evening. Franklin, Gerry, and the boys also came.

Sat 8 – Fair very warm. Irwin & the boys went nutting. Franklin, Geo & Richard and I went to Belleville to Streck's. Bill, Anita and June came towards evening.

Sun 9 – Fair very warm. Viola, Ralph, Katie and the 3 children came for dinner. Mary & Irv and children were at the Denmark farm for dinner. Bill, Anita, & June and Edwin, Beulah, and the girls came in afternoon. *Edwin Dintelmann is George's nephew.*

Mon 10 – Partly cloudy strong south winds, rain by night. Franklin and family left for home at eight o'clock and Irwin & Mary left at noon. Rained all night, very warm.

Tues 11 – Rained all day. We were at Millstadt to pay church supper bills. Then had a committee meeting in the evening. Cleared $443.

Wed 12 – Fair cooler very pretty day. I washed and ironed and picked some apples.

Thurs 13 – Fair very pretty day. I ironed and picked apples and worked about the yard. Were to Grange meeting in evening.

Fri 14 – Another pretty day. We both worked about the place. I potted more flowers. Geo made firewood.

Sat 15 – Cooler to cloudy. I sowed winter lettuce and helped Geo with the firewood. Celebrated Lena Klein's birthday in evening.

Sun 16 – Very pretty day. Were at church. Afternoon I was at the consistory meeting. In evening Schillings were here.

Mon 17 – Fair warm 56 degrees. We were at our Home Bureau meeting at the home of Mrs. Henry Stahlman.

Tues 18 – Fair to cloudy warm. Clara and I were at Leo Wachtel's to visit Mrs. Peter Wachtel. Schillings started to sow wheat in 7 acres.

Wed 19 – Cloudy rain all day from 11:30 a.m. on. Schillings finished wheat on our land. Louis sowed some too. I was at convention at Millstadt church.

Thurs 20 – Rain mostly all day. We and Orville Koerbers were at Boobie Klein's in evening.

Fri 21 – Rain all day. I patched and sewed. Geo mixed feed.

Sat 22 – Cold windy all day. Put on our storm windows.

Sun 23 – 48 degrees, very cloudy. We and Metzgers were at Oswald Etling's this afternoon.

Mon 24 – Cloudy cold all day, 48 in morning. We made firewood and I hauled it into the brooder house.

Tues 25 – Cloudy to fair 47 degrees. Edgar, Toddy & children & Katie were here in morning. Clara and Ronald's wife were here afternoon. *Edgar Luetzelschwab is Katie's nephew.*

Wed 26 – Fair cool. I baked cookies. Geo made firewood. Irwin came in the evening and stayed overnight.

Thurs 27 – Fair heavy frost 27 degrees. Irwin left for home this morning. This evening I had to put on the program at the Grange.

Fri 28 – Fair 35 degrees, white frost. I have to dress chicken and get things ready to go to Urbana tomorrow.

Sat 29 – Fair warm, very pretty day. I was overnight at Bill & Anita's and we all went to Urbana this morning. Mary & Irwin were there too.

Sun 30 – Fair very pretty day. We all enjoyed Franklin's birthday supper last night. Spent the evening in seeing pictures. Then had music & singing. We left for home at 9:45 a.m. Got to Bill's place at 1:30. Came home about 4:30.

Mon 31 – Fair strong NW winds, cold 27. Robert Franke took our hogs to Streck's, 5 weighted 1,590 lbs. We got $16.60.

November 1949

Tues 1 – Fair cold down to 24 degrees. Geo made firewood and I dug up cannas and brought wood in the basement.

Wed 2 – Cold 27 degrees. We were at Millstadt and also got molasses from Herman and Frank. *Herman and Frank Luetzelschwab are Katie's brothers who never married and lived together on the Luetzelschwab homestead which was a double log cabin, barn, and outbuildings.*

Thurs 3 – Fair some warmer. We had Grange meeting this evening.

Fri 4 – Fair some warmer. We worked about the place. Were at Guild meeting in evening. I gave the program.

Sat 5 – Fair very pretty day cool. I did my Saturday work. Geo mixed feed.

Sun 6 – Fair beautiful day. Willie, Anita and June Ann were here for dinner. We were at Gus Metzger's birthday party in evening.

Mon 7 – Fair warmer no frost. I washed and carried in wood. Geo gathered corn.

Tues 8 – Fair warm 40 degrees. Roushes took us along to the Farm Bureau meeting and dinner.

Wed 9 – Fair 42 degrees much warmer, during the day strong winds SW. I was at Schilling's a little while.

Thurs 10 – Fair very warm. We were at Millstadt had a horn put on the truck also got Anita's rag rug and we were at Woodland Grange in evening.

Fri 11 – Fair very warm 59 in morning, 78 by afternoon, windy. I worked about the house and baked coffee cake.

Sat 12 – Cloudy heavy dew, south winds, still warm, thundering and light rain by night.

Sun 13 – Fair cooler. I was at church. Henry & Bertha, John & Audry, Bill & Anita & June, Elmer & Carolina and Christie were here for dinner. *Henry and John Reiss are George's brothers. Bertha is Henry's wife and Audry is John's daughter. Bill Reiss is George and Katie's son, and Carolina Gumersheimer is Katie's sister.*

Mon 14 – Fair. We worked about the place.

Tues 15 – Fair warmer. I cleaned off the patch by the shed. In evening we were at Turkey Hill Grange with Kleins to see the degree work.

Wed 16 – Very stormy and much colder, fair. We made some firewood and hauled it in.

Thurs 17 – Fair 35 very stormy. We brought in more wood and I did some cleaning in the basement. Were at Boobie's birthday party in the evening.

Fri 18 – Fair cold 29 ice on water. We cleaned the chicken house and put straw in.

Sat 19 – Fair. We worked about the place. I baked a birthday cake.

Sun 20 – Fair to cloudy. Bill, Anita & June Ann and Mr. Keenan were here for supper. They took us to Frank Klein's birthday party. *Mr. Keenan is Bill's boss at Socony Oil in East St. Louis and his occasional hunting partner.*

Mon 21 – Fair. We cleaned the chicken house and worked about the place.

Tues 22 – Fair. We made firewood. In evening we went to the Smithton card party with Metzgers. I won a nice white dish pan.

Wed 23 – Fair warmer. We went to Broad Hollow Grange card party with Metzgers. Geo won a prize.

Thurs 24 – Fair, not too cold, cloudy by night and rain & snow flurries while we went to Grange meeting with Metzgers. Election of officers.

Fri 25 – Fair cold and windy all day, 27 degrees in morning. We made more firewood.

Sat 26 – Fair to partly cloudy, cold 30 degrees. Roy took us to Bill and Anita's house at 6:30 in morning. We went to Irwin & Mary's with Bill & Anita.

Sun 27 – Fair frost but getting warmer. We left Irwin's house at one o'clock noon got home at 5:30 evening.

Mon 28 – Fair very warm no frost. We cleaned the chicken house and put straw in it. Schilling's boys came in evening & fixed the electric oven.

Tues 29 – Fair very warm. We were at Millstadt and then at Smithton. Got a new battery in our coupe today. Clemence Reinhardt brought it.

Wed 30 – Fair warm. We made firewood and also cleaned along the road between us and Klein's.

December 1949

Thurs 1 – Fair we worked about the place.

Fri 2 – Fair around 35 degrees. We made firewood. Were at the play of the Grange at Floraville in evening.

Sat 3 – Fair to cloudy light rain by night. We worked about the place all day.

Sun 4 – Fair very pretty day, 32 degrees in early morning. We were at Bill & Anita's for June Ann's 13th birthday.

Mon 5 – Fair 32 degrees. We made firewood and burned brush. Kleins took us to the tax meeting in evening.

Tues 6 – Fair to cloudy light shower. We brought in wood and filled feather pillows. Were at Marcella's in the evening.

Wed 7 – Fair to cloudy 44 degrees getting colder. We burned brush in the chicken yard and made more firewood.

Thurs 8 – Cold 21 degrees warmed up some during the day. We went to the Grange meeting with Metzgers.

Fri 9 – Cold 22 degrees, cloudy all day, snow and rain toward evening.

Sat 10 – 35 degrees rainy all day. I did quite a bit sewing, made sheets and sewed carpet rags.

Sun 11 – Fair very warm 71 degrees by 3 o'clock. Herman & Frank were here for dinner. I was at church in the morning, gave a report.

Mon 12 – Fair to cloudy 33 degrees. I washed. In evening we went to Belleville with Boobie & Marcella to the meeting at the junior high school.

Tues 13 – 20 degrees, fair to cloudy. I was at Roush's for a few hours in evening. I ironed and patched.

Wed 14 – Fair, our coldest day 19 above. Patsy and I were at Belleville to take the Home Bureau lesson. We were at Broad Hollow Grange officers' installation.

Thurs 15 – Colder 15 above, fair. I cleaned the rooms and got beds ready for Mary & Irwin when they come for the holidays.

Fri 16 – 24 degrees, fair warmer. We were at Millstadt and to the funeral of Charles Deash.

Sat 17 – 39 degrees, cloudy rain by noon. We made quite a bit of firewood and put it into the basement.

Sun 18 – Fair. Irwin, Mary & children came towards evening to stay thru till Christmas.

Mon 19 – Irwin left to go to the southern farms, getting cloudy and rainy.

Tues 20 – Rain almost all night, fair during the day. Pop & I went to oil meeting with Roushes. In evening we were at Oscar Koerber's birthday party.

Wed 21 – Rainy all day & night. Irwin came home by evening. We enjoyed having Mary & the children for the week.

Thurs 22 – Cloudy cold & ugly. We all went to the Grange pot luck supper and stayed for the Xmas program.

Fri 23 – Fair very pretty day. We all drove to Waterloo. Irwin had to go to the bank. Afternoon Irv & Mary went to St. Louis to buy shoes. Opened our gifts in evening.

Sat 24 – Fair. Franklin & family came by noon and Bill, Anita & June came by evening, had supper with us, then we all went to church in evening.

Sun 25 – Fair warm. We all went to Bill & Anita's for Xmas dinner. Franklin & family were there also. We all enjoyed the day very much.

Mon 26 – Very cloudy and foggy, no frost. Irv & Mary and the children left for home by noon. Boobie & Marcella & children were here in evening.

Tues 27 – Fair 30 degrees, but warmed up nicely. Geo got stuck with the truck in orchard while spreading fertilizer. Schillings came in evening.

Wed 28 – Fair light frost in morning, 54 by noon. I had a bad cold so I didn't do much work.

Thurs 29 – Warm very pretty day. I patched and worked on the road a little. We got 5 loads of road rock to fill in bad places.

Fri 30 – Fair very pretty day. I still had a cold so I stayed in the house till noon. Then we made some firewood out by the 7 acres.

Sat 31 – 54 degrees, light rain at times. I patched. Geo mixed feed.

1950

January 1950

Sun 1 – Very cloudy & foggy, warm 50. We were at church and then spent the day at home.

Mon 2 – Warm 58 degrees rainy all day. I still have my cold. Uncle Will spent the day with us.

Tues 3 – 61 degrees, rained hard thru the night, also thundered. Very heavy rain and bad storm. Our basement is full of water.

Wed 4 – Very much colder 16 above, snowing & sleeting. After an all night downpour of rain. Basement had more water than ever before.

Thurs 5 – Fair to cloudy 10 above. Geo did the feeding. I sewed rags for carpets and patched. Sleeted quite a lot thru the night.

Fri 6 – 20 degrees, sleeting at times, all we can do is feeding and the house work.

Sat 7 – 22 degrees, fair thawing. I worked about the house. Geo did the feeding.

Sun 8 – Fair 28 degrees. This is Sunday but we stayed home & I worked on my lesson.

Mon 9 – Fair warmer 45 degrees got very muddy. I washed a large wash and ironed in evening.

Tues 10 – Fair windy very warm 46 in morning, very muddy. We took eggs and young roosters to Millstadt. Eggs 26 cents and rooster .18 a lb.

Wed 11 – 25 degrees cloudy. Geo is making firewood. I'm sewing. In evening we went to Robert Probst's birthday party with Metzgers.

Thurs 12 – Rainy and warmer. I cleaned the beds. We were at Grange meeting in the evening. Rained slowly all night. Going to have a card party Feb 16.

Fri 13 – Rain 66 degrees. Patsy came and we worked on our lesson. Clearing by evening and colder.

Sat 14 – 25 degrees fair. We worked about the place. Geo went to telephone meeting in afternoon. Rain by night.

Sun 15 – 67 degrees rainy, clearing late afternoon and much colder.

Mon 16 – 18 above fair, very pretty day. I had the Home Bureau meeting here with 28 present. Patsy and I gave the major lesson.

Tues 17 – It was 30 degrees fair to cloudy by night. I went to Belleville with Frank Kleins to make income report. Paid 69 dollars.

Wed 18 – 20 above, cloudy cold NW winds. We stayed in the house all day. It didn't go above 20 all day.

Thurs 19 – Cold 25 degrees, fair. We got a load of wood out of the woods here and then I sewed quilt patches.

Fri 20 – Fair cold 28 degrees. We butchered today. John Rapp helped us. Brother Johnnie Luetzelschwab was here and said Katie is sick.

Sat 21 – Fair 35 degrees. We got a load of wood for the furnace and then I rendered the lard. It made 7 gallons.

Sun 22 – Cloudy 48 degrees. We were at church. Then Bill, Anita & June came for dinner. We played cards at Klein's in evening.

Mon 23 – Very foggy and cloudy 57 degrees. We took meat to the locker. Also took eggs along, got 26 a doz. We visited with Katie Luetzelschwab. She is in bed. *Katie is the wife of Katie's brother John Luetzelschwab.*

Tues 24 – Partly cloudy 62 degrees, 75 degrees by afternoon, very windy from south. I was quilting at Marcella's.

Wed 25 – Fair to cloudy 69 to 75 degrees very stormy from the south, thundershowers by night. I helped Marcella quilt in the afternoon. Heavy rain at night.

Thurs 26 – Fair much colder 25 at 6 a.m., 21 by noon, stormy. We had Grange meeting and quilting instead of a program. 20 degrees at midnight.

Fri 27 – Fair 20 above, 34 by noon. I quilted at Floraville, then I took one home and the other quilt we took to Clara Mehrmann.

Sat 28 – 34 degrees, warmed up fast, cloudy 56 by evening. Geo made firewood. I did my Saturday work and quilted.

Sun 29 – Cloudy 53 degrees at 7 a.m., wind turned to northwest and in 2 hours, it was down to 30, and 20 by 4 p.m., still getting colder.

Mon 30 – Very cloudy 18 degrees, warmed up to 24 during the day, sleet and some snow fell towards evening.

Tues 31 – 20 degrees, sleet and ice all over but not on trees. Kleins got us to go along to Mike Mueth's quilting in evening.

February 1950

Wed 1 – 24 degrees, cloudy. I quilted on my quilt, stayed cold all day.

Thurs 2 – Fair for the ground hog. 20 degrees but warmed up to 35 degrees. Ladies came and finished my quilt in the evening.

Fri 3 – 25 degrees but warmed up to 44. We took the eggs to Millstadt and visited John and Katie, she was sitting up.

Sat 4 – Fair. We hauled a load of furnace wood up and then I did my Saturday work.

Sun 5 – Cloudy to fair. We were at Henry and Edna's for dinner and lunch. It thawed and got very muddy. 51 degrees. *Edna Lang is Katie's sister. Henry plants and harvests some of the Reiss' crops.*

Mon 6 – 50 cloudy all day, 55 degrees. I washed. Turned cooler toward evening. Geo made firewood.

Tues 7 – 48 degrees, cloudy to fair. We worked in woods by rye pasture. I was to a church quilting in evening.

Wed 8 – 43 degrees, very cloudy, lightninged but didn't rain. I sewed. Geo made firewood and mixed feed.

Thurs 9 – Fair to cloudy, 30 degrees. I worked on remodeling old clothes. Grange meeting in evening.

Fri 10 – Fair very pretty day, 33 degrees. We took the eggs to Millstadt, then I worked around the house, visited Gus & Alma. Quilted at Klein's.

Sat 11 – Fair 34 degrees, white frost. I did my Saturday work and brought in firewood.

Sun 12 – Rained all day and all night, creeks were out. We spent the Sunday at home all day.

Mon 13 – Rain & sleet, much colder, was slick to walk, very stormy, came down to 19 above.

Tues 14 – Fair cold, very stormy. I sewed all day and George stayed in the house too.

Wed 15 – Fair cold 20 degrees, windy. I quilted on the baby quilt.

Thurs 16 – 22 degrees, fair, very pretty day. We had our Grange card party this evening, good crowd. Cleared $335.

Fri 17 – 24 degrees, fair. I helped Lena Klein quilt, afternoon & evening. We got some furnace wood from the woods in the morning.

Sat 18 – 34 degrees. I did my Saturday work and quilted on Elsie Hesse's baby quilt. *Elsie is the younger sister of Katie's daughter-in-law, Anita Hesse Reiss.*

Sun 19 – Fair 24 degrees. We were at church. Bill, Anita & June were here for dinner. In evening we were at Marcella's birthday party.

Mon 20 – 30 degrees, fair, very pretty day. Mrs. Roush and I were to the Home Bureau meeting at Germann's.

Tues 21 – Rained hard mostly all day. Eileen Grau and I went to Rapp's quilting in early morning. Franklin & family came towards evening. Creeks out.

Wed 22 – Light snow to fair. Franklin, Gerry, and the boys left for home at 9 o'clock in the morning. I set up a quilt of old feed sacks.

Thurs 23 – Fair 32 degrees. Irwin came at 8 o'clock in morning and left again at one o'clock noon.

Fri 24 – 22 degrees, fair. We took eggs to Smithton. Afternoon I quilted. Geo made firewood.

Sat 25 – Fair 20 degrees. I quilted and baked bread & cake. Geo mixed feed. Jacob Wachtel was buried today.

Sun 26 – Fair, cold 10 above. We went to the church hall to prepare for the birthday supper in the evening. It warmed up to 34 during the day.

Mon 27 – Fair to cloudy & warmer, southeast wind. We butchered today and I cooked the lard in the evening.

Tues 28 – Fair after a hard rain last night. We took the meat to the locker. Then Mrs. Roush came and we finished the quilt.

March 1950

Wed 1 – Fair colder 30 degrees, stormy, northwest winds, very cold and very stormy all day and night. I set up a quilt.

Thurs 2 – 10 above, not so stormy any more. I had a quilting afternoon and evening. There were 7 of us in afternoon and 5 in evening.

Fri 3 – Fair warmer, 23 degrees. I quilted, Geo made firewood. We went to the Guild meeting in evening.

Sat 4 – Fair 32 degrees, but warmed up to 45, was a very pretty day. Did my Saturday work. Geo crushed & shelled corn.

Sun 5 – Fair, a most beautiful day, warmed up to 70 degrees by noon. We were at church, then to Roush's and at Metzger's in the evening.

Mon 6 – 40 degrees, fair 70 by noon, stormy. We worked on the road by Klein's and I raked some in the yard.

Tues 7 – Fair to cloudy getting colder by night, very stormy from southwest. One could hardly be outside. We got some posts at Roush's.

Wed 8 – Snow flurries to fair and very stormy 18 degrees. Franklin came in the afternoon. He went to Shiloh Valley Grange in evening.

Thurs 9 – 22 degrees, fair. Franklin left for home at noon. Then I quilted and Geo mixed feed.

Fri 10 – 30 degrees, fair, getting warmer. I quilted. Geo made firewood.

Sat 11 – 44 degrees, cloudy rain towards evening and rained all night.

Sun 12 – Raining and freezing, ice on trees and fences, 30 degrees. We stayed home all day.

Mon 13 – 21 degrees, snow flurries, trees & wire fences full of ice, although none on ground, fair by noon, colder by night. I cleaned drawers & shelves.

Tues 14 – 24 degrees, fair, warmed up to 45 by noon. Mike Mueth's took us along to Broad Hollow Grange card party.

Wed 15 – Rain afternoon & evening. I worked in the basement.

Thurs 16 – 40 degrees, cloudy to fair and colder. Nora & Edward Kempf took us along to Shiloh Grange for Pomona meeting. We joined.

Fri 17 – 32 degrees, fair, warmed up to 50 by noon. We got fence for our yard, also took eggs to Smithton.

Sat 18 – 30 degrees, fair to cloudy, cold east winds. Got a load of road rock by the cedar trees back of feed house. Bill, Anita, & June were here for supper.

Sun 19 – Cloudy, 40 degrees. We were at church. Started to rain towards evening. The birthday card came for my birthday ahead of time.

Mon 20 – Cloudy all day. Patsy and I went to the Home Bureau meeting at Kayson's.

Tues 21 – Foggy cloudy to fair and getting colder. We took eggs & chickens to Millstadt. Eggs 27, hens 24 ½ a lb. Geo & Boobie went to a school meeting in evening.

Wed 22 – 35 degrees, cold windy with a few snowflakes, then fair. Henry & boys were here to start building my yard fence. Lavern painted the kitchen.

Thurs 23 – Fair 32 degrees, then warm, southeast wind. I washed. Grange meeting in evening. Irwin, Mary, and the children will come tomorrow.

Fri 24 – Cold winds, fair. Henry and the boys worked on the yard fence, tore down the old brooder house and set new posts. Irwin & Mary and family came.

Sat 25 – Fair, windy, and getting warmer. Henry, Harold and Lavern cut down the big wind charger pole and put up a telephone pole for the private line. *Harold and Lavern Lang are Henry's sons. All three were very helpful to the Reisses.*

Sun 26 – Fair very warm. Henry, Bill, Anita and June Ann were here. It was up to 76 degrees for a while, thunderstorm by night, hard rain.

Mon 27 – Cloudy to fair. Mary & Irwin and children left for home this morning. We started taking down the old yard fence.

Tues 28 – Fair very stormy & cold. Henry & Harold Lang finished our yard fence. Lavern painted our kitchen walls & ceiling.

Wed 29 – Fair very stormy, cold but no frost. We cleared away the old brooder house boards and posts.

Thurs 30 – Fair cold 31 in morning, white frost. We worked about the outside yard.

Fri 31 – 44 degrees, very cloudy, started to rain hard by evening. We made firewood and worked about the yard.

April 1950

Sat 1 – 38 degrees, party cloudy, NW winds. I worked about the yard and did my Saturday work. Geo mixed feed.

Sun 2 – Rain mostly all day and night. We went to church at Waterloo to Harvey Hoffman's confirmation, then to Elsie Hoffman's house for dinner.

Mon 3 – Cloudy with showers off and on during the day. 70 by 3 PM. Lavern finished painting our kitchen. Electric went off by 5:15 and by 7 to nine o'clock, we had bad thundering and rain.

Tues 4 – Clearing and colder 43 by noon, creeks were out last night. I worked about the house.

Wed 5 – Cloudy & cold, couldn't do much outside work. I did a lot of cleaning in the house.

Thurs 6 – Cloudy & cold to fair & warmer. We worked about the yard. The ladies came and we practiced our skit for the Pomona meeting.

Fri 7 – Fair very pretty day warm. This was Good Friday. Lavern came and finished painting my kitchen.

Sat 8 – Fair very pretty day, warm 60 to 70 degrees. We worked about the yard and I baked coffee cake.

Sun 9 – 53 degrees cloudy rain by evening. Easter Sunday. We were at church. Afternoon the Roush boys brought me an Easter lily.

Mon 10 – Fair 45 degrees to 57, very stormy from south, rain by evening. I washed today and ironed.

Tues 11 – 38 degrees, very cloudy & stormy, NW winds. We went voting and then took eggs to Smithton, only got 25 cents a dozen.

Wed 12 – Cloudy getting colder, very stormy 35 degrees, snow flurries. Pomona meeting at Floraville. We put on the skit. Betsy joins the Grange.

Thurs 13 – 26 degrees, very stormy from NW, partly cloudy. We were at Millstadt Grange meeting in evening.

Fri 14 – 25 degrees but warmed up fast and was a pretty day, NW wind. We worked about the place. Grange play in evening. Franklin, Gerry & boys came.

Sat 15 – Fair, white frost, very pretty day. Franklin took us all to Belleville, then to John & Katie at Millstadt. Afternoon they walked around. *John Luetzelschwab is Katie's brother.*

Sun 16 – Fair very pretty day. We all went to Bill & Anita's for dinner. Anita had a beautiful cake for our 39th wedding anniversary. Franklin & Gerry left for home.

Mon 17 – Cloudy to fair warm. Mrs. Roush and I were at the Home Bureau meeting at Mrs. Glauber's. Geo & I were at the Grange play last night.

Tues 18 – Fair very warm, very pretty day. I planted a lot of cannas & iris. Went to Paderborn card party in evening.

Wed 19 – 53 degrees in morning, rained a little during early morning, clearing after 6 AM. Irwin came in evening, stayed over night.

Thurs 20 – Fair cool 45. Irwin left at eleven o'clock. I started cleaning the brooder house and planted weigelia shrubs from Mary.

Fri 21 – Fair to partly cloudy, light shower. I cleaned the brooder house and we set up the brooder. Also planted crepe myrtle.

Sat 22 – Fair, hot 85 degrees by noon. I worked in the garden all day. Geo hauled some ground in the yard. Light shower.

Sun 23 – Fair beautiful day, warmed up to 86 by noon. Got my hair fixed at Brandenburger's. Henry & Bertha were here and birthday club in the evening. *Henry Reiss is George's brother from St. Louis.*

Mon 24 – 71 degrees at 6 a.m., fair. We took eggs & roosters to Smithton, eggs 26 & roosters 16 a lb. Howertons paid 4 dollars pasture rent to May 24.

Tues 25 – Fair warm. Got 100 chicks today. I worked in garden, planted beans. Were at Smithton card party with Metzgers. Cool by night.

Wed 26 – Fair warm but cool at night. I planted some mail order shrubs from Henry Fields. Went to Brennen show at Floraville, got prize for longest married couple.

Thurs 27 – 42 degrees, cloudy to fair, stayed cold all day. Finished planting the shrubs from Fields. Grange meeting in evening.

Fri 28 – 41 degrees, cloudy & showery, hard rain by night and all night. I planted cannas and glads.

Sat 29 – 48 degrees raining slowly all day. I worked about the house and did my Saturday work.

Sun 30 – Very cloudy all day, misty at times. Mr. & Mrs. Hesse, Mr. & Mrs. Roland Heidenreich, and Bill, Anita and June Ann were here.

May 1950

Mon 1 – Partly cloudy 48 degrees. I washed then we took eggs to Smithton.

Tues 2 – Partly cloudy all day. I planted dahlias and cannas also roses and shrubs from Wards.

Wed 3 – Partly cloudy to fair 85 degrees. I worked in the garden till noon, then I went to Schilling's awhile towards evening. I pulled weeds.

Thurs 4 – Partly cloudy all day. I spaded in the garden. Afternoon we went to Roush's a while. Then Geo mixed feed and I planted flower seeds.

Fri 5 – Very stormy from southeast, shifting to west by night & cooler up to 80 during day, no rain. We got 300 baby chicks today.

Sat 6 – Fair 61 degrees warmed up to 75 during noon, cool again at night. I sowed lettuce. Mrs. Roush was here to get flowers.

Sun 7 – Fair, very pretty day. We were at church. Afternoon Henry and Edna were here. Evening we were at Boobie & Marcella's.

Mon 8 – Cloudy. I was at Belleville with Schillings. Afternoon Mr. & Mrs. Edwin Joseph were here. I spaded some in the garden. *The Josephs would soon replace the Howerton family as the Reiss farm tenants who also lived in the older homestead house built in 1889.*

Tues 9 – Thundershowers. I worked in the house. Started to rain steady by 4 o'clock and rained all night.

Wed 10 – Still raining slowly, cloudy all day, rain by midnight. Kempfs took us along to Bluff Grange to Pomona meeting.

Thurs 11 – Raining and rained all day. We went to Paderborn church for Betty's wedding then I stayed at Klein's. Went to Grange meeting in evening.

Fri 12 – Fair warm. I went to New Athens with Howertons. Afternoon we took eggs to Millstadt. Late in the evening, Mary, Irv and children came.

Sat 13 – Fair, very pretty day. We all went to see Aunt Katie. In evening Bill, Anita & June Ann came. We had supper together.

Sun 14 – Fair after a little shower. Irwin, Mary, and Mary Kay left for California. The boys are with us. I canned 8 pints pineapples. We paid our 1949 church dues, $10 to Bill Kempf.

Mon 15 – Fair, very pretty day. Patsy came and took me and the boys to the Home Bureau meeting at Miss Ogle's. Irwin called in evening from Colorado.

Tues 16 – Fair hot. The boys and I cut and pulled weeds and I baked rolls. Geo took a case of eggs to Smithton.

Wed 17 – Fair hot. We cleaned the chicken house and hoed weeds.

Thurs 18 – Cool, fair. I planted more dahlias and cannas and we cleaned the chicken house, also cut weeds.

Fri 19 – Cloudy quite a bit of rain by afternoon. We cleaned chicken house in morning.

Sat 20 – Fair hot 85 degrees. We cleaned the chicken house and put weeds in for litter.

Sun 21 – Partly cloudy to fair and cooler by night. We and the boys were at church. Then we had a lot of company in afternoon.

Mon 22 – Fair hot 87 during noon, cool in early morning. I chopped weeds and worked in the garden.

Tues 23 – 76 degrees at 6 a.m., hotter during the day. I chopped weeds, spaded, and sowed flower seeds.

Wed 24 – Hot. I cut weeds and spaded more in the front garden. Clarence Louis started plowing for corn.

Thurs 25 – Fair hot. Clarence Louis is here working on his corn land.

Fri 26 – Very hot today with a heavy rain storm by night. Henry Lang plowed sheep pasture. Louis planted his corn here. *The "sheep pasture" was eight acres on the east side of the barn. The Reisses no longer raised sheep but the name stuck for that field.*

Sat 27 – Fair. I baked rolls and coffee cake also an angle food cake and picked 2 qts strawberries.

Sun 28 – Fair. We took the boys to Sunday School. Then Bill, Anita & June came for dinner. Then we all went to Hesse's. Irwin called from Los Angeles.

Mon 29 – Rain late afternoon and at night. Henry Lang started to mow clover. I hoed out weeds and picked 2 qts strawberries.

Tues 30 – Partly cloudy, cooler. I picked 3 qts strawberries in the orchard. We cooked 6 glasses strawberry jelly and froze 3 qts.

Wed 31 – Fair cool. I mowed lawn, pulled weeds and picked strawberries.

June 1950

Thurs 1 – Fair cool. I washed and picked berries and cleaned some of the rooms.

Fri 2 – Fair cool in morning, hot later and stormy. I cleaned the rooms and ironed & patched.

Sat 3 – Rain all day till about 4 o'clock afternoon. Mary, Irv and Mary Kay came back from Calif. at 6 o'clock. Stevie & Ken were happy.

Sun 4 – Fair cool. Bill & Anita were here. In evening Geo & I were at Alma's birthday party.

Mon 5 – Fair cool, very pretty day. Mary & Irwin & children left for Sullivan in afternoon. Now we are lonesome.

Tues 6 – Fair. I worked about the yard and picked the strawberries.

Wed 7 – Fair. I washed and in the afternoon I went to Waterloo with the Guild ladies.

Thurs 8 – Fair. We took eggs to Smithton. Then Geo mixed feed. I mowed the lawn, picked the last strawberries.

Fri 9 – Showers. We were at Millstadt. Then I worked in the garden.

Sat 10 – Fair. I baked rolls and then Geo & I went to Albert Hoffman's.

Sun 11 – Fair cool, beautiful day. We and Alma & Gus went to the Smithton Sunday school program and picnic at Broad Hollow Grange.

Mon 12 – 66 degrees in morning, 80 later on, fair. I aired and cleaned the winter suits and put them away for the summer. Clara was here afternoon.

Tues 13 – 67 degrees in morning. Rained very hard by afternoon. I worked in the brooder house shed, cleaned it.

Wed 14 – 70 degrees morning, 90 by noon. Roushes came to ask to lease pasture land. Then I quilted at Wachtel's. Bill, Anita & June came in evening. *Roushes lived a quarter mile south, next to the Schilling's. The Roushes also had three sons who were very helpful to the Reisses.*

Thurs 15 – 71 degrees in early morning, 92 by noon, fair. We didn't do very much today. We were at Roush's.

Fri 16 – 77 degrees at six o'clock in morning, fair, 92 by noon. The Joseph's were here today to see the farm and rent it.

Sat 17 – 65 degrees, very cloudy, rained lightly in the night. I remodeled dresses and patched. We told Mrs. Howerton today they had to move.

Sun 18 – Fair, hot all day. I baked pies & cake. Bill, Anita and June were here in evening.

Mon 19 – 66 degrees, cool all day. Mrs. Roush & I were at the Home Bureau meeting at Mrs. Simon's. It was very cloudy all day.

Tues 20 – 67 degrees, hard shower in forenoon. We were at Waterloo at Mary's. Afternoon I baked rolls and worked in garden. Joseph's were here.

Wed 21 – Cool in morning. We went to Waterloo again to exchange the meat scraps. Then we went to Smithton to have the move notice written.

Thurs 22 – Fair, hot all day. I pulled weeds. Also helped Joseph's a short while to clean up the hog lot. Written notice today to R. Howerton.

Fri 23 – 70 at 6 a.m. Geo and I started on building the chicken yard fence and I pulled weeds in the yard.

Sat 24 – 78 degrees at 6 a.m., 94 by noon. John & Katie and Mr. & Mrs. Roush and Romauld were here. We set fence posts.

Sun 25 – Fair hot winds 93 degrees at 6 p.m. Henry Lang and Alma Mueller were here today. We spent Sunday at home.

Mon 26 – Fair 82 degrees at 6 a.m., 94 by noon. We were at Smithton to send bank draft to pay fertilizer. I finished darning socks & then mowed lawn.

Tues 27 – 70 degrees, cloudy. Chopped weeds. Helped Marcella put up sauerkraut.

Wed 28 – Very cool 64 degrees, cloudy & rainy. Clear by evening. Geo mixed feed. Rapps came and picked the cherries.

Thurs 29 – 62 degrees, fair. I baked cookies and worked about the place.

Fri 30 – 62 in morning, 85 afternoon. Schillings brought one hopper full of wheat but it was too damp yet. Geo & I cleaned upstairs barn.

July 1950

Sat 1 – 65 degrees, fair, rained a hard shower by 3 o'clock. Mary & Irwin & children came after the rain.

Sun 2 – Fair. Mary & Irv & Pop set some fence posts. Bill, Anita, June and Uncle Henry were here for dinner. *Henry Reiss is George's brother from St. Louis.*

Mon 3 – 65 degrees, fair, getting hot. Irwin & Pop went to the Farms. Mary & I took down the storm windows. We all were at Bill & Anita's for supper.

Tues 4 – Cloudy 68 degrees, rained hard last night. Irv & Mary and children left for home this morning. The Josephs were here this afternoon.

Wed 5 – Fair 64 degrees.

Thurs 6 – 64 degrees, fair, stayed cool all day. We hauled 2 loads of wheat today, $1.20 and $1.35 for old garlic wheat.

Fri 7 – 62 degrees, fair. I started to clean the feed house. Got it about half done.

Sat 8 – 68 degrees, hot during noon. We mixed a lot of feed and cleaned feed house.

Sun 9 – 69 degrees in early morning, hot during day. We spent Sunday at home. Louis came & brought us wheat & check for $216.06 for wheat.

Mon 10 – 68, warmed up to 88. We mixed more feed. Josephs brought some wheat over. I also mowed a lot of weeds.

Tues 11 – 67, warmed up to 90 by afternoon. We moved our oats out of the barn bin. Joseph brought his oats in.

Wed 12 – Very hot all day, 97 for a while. I patched, couldn't do much outdoors.

Thurs 13 – Very cool & cloudy all day. Mrs. Westerheide and Charles were here all day. We picked the first blackberries today.

Fri 14 – 55 degrees in early morning. I worked about the place. Roland & Elsie and baby Heidenreich were here. *Elsie is Anita Reiss' sister. The baby is Rosemarie.*

Sat 15 – 58 in early morning, hot later with hot SW winds. I did my Saturday work. Franklin, Gerry & boys came by noon.

Sun 16 – Cloudy, light shower. Franklin went back by bus and Gerry & boys will stay this week. Had float meeting in afternoon.

Mon 17 – Fair. I was sick so I didn't get any work done. Gerry and boys came back from Bill & Anita's in the evening.

Tues 18 – Fair, warmer. We all went to Viola & Ralph's for dinner and to Beulah's for supper. John, Lillian & girls were there also. *Viola Bald and Beulah Dintelmann are George's nieces. John Reiss is George's brother in Sikeston, Missouri. Lillian is John's daughter who has two daughters of her own, Jo Ellen and Katy.*

Wed 19 – Fair. We all went to Edna & Henry, then to John & Katie's for dinner. Toddy & Edgar and children were there. *John Luetzelschwab is Katie's brother. Edgar is John's son.*

Thurs 20 – Cloudy and cooler. Gerry, I and the boys took chickens to Millstadt, then went to Carlena's and then to Elsie & Albert Hoffman's. To Roush's for supper.

Fri 21 – Cool 68 degrees. We stayed home and prepared supper for Edgar & family. John & Katie and Bill & Anita and June also Tillie Rahe and Bobbie came.

Sat 22 – Cool. We went to Waterloo on business. June Ann stayed here with George & Richard. Then Gerry went to Anita's and got Franklin at station.

Sun 23 – Cool, fair. We all were at the Paderborn picnic last night. Bill & Anita were here for dinner. Franklin and family left for home afternoon.

Mon 24 – Fair, hot 87 degrees at noon. Brother John & Katie were here. The men fixed the hay fork and put concrete in the shop. We sold 112 bu corn $1.50.

Tues 25 – 58 degrees at six a.m., fair. We shelled and ground corn and mixed feed. Afternoon I went to Schilling's for a short while.

Wed 26 – 60 degrees in morning light drizzle. Geo & Joseph took a load of corn to mill and then got tin roofing at East St. Louis. Ted Klein filled ground in the buggy shed.

Thurs 27 – 56 degrees, foggy, fair. We sold another load of corn 38 bu @$1.50. Afternoon we were at Louis Etling's sale. Evening at Grange meeting.

Fri 28 – Fair, hot. We cleaned up the corn cobs, picked blackberries. We are going to the Smithton home coming with our Grange float tomorrow.

Sat 29 – Fair not so hot. Smithton had a large parade and many pretty floats.

Sun 30 – Fair. We were at church then went to Smithton picnic with Metzgers. Stayed home in evening.

Mon 31 – 78 degrees in early morning. I washed. Had a good rain by afternoon. Irwin came in the evening.

August 1950

Tues 1 – Light shower in early morning then partly cloudy & hot. Irwin left for Springfield and we hauled oats out of the barn.

Wed 2 – Fair cool 66 in morning. We went to the Belleville Fair with Metzgers. We stayed for the evening.

Thurs 3 – Cool fair 64 degrees. We cleaned up in the shed over on the other place. Josephs brought more tools.

Fri 4 – Cool 53 degrees. We went to Belleville with Joseph to see about things here also called Franklin. Guild meeting, I gave program.

Sat 5 – 68 degrees but warmed up much by noon. Ludger fixed the truck. Josephs & Reinhardts were here. *Ludger is one of the Schilling's sons from half a mile south.*

Sun 6 – Fair 69 in early morning. We were at the Woodman's picnic. Bill, Anita, June were here for a short while. Mr. Keller was here in evening.

Mon 7 – 62 degrees fair hot by afternoon. We were at the field day meeting at Hugo Hearthing's all day.

Tues 8 – Rained mostly all day, cool. We paid our taxes today $302.56. Mrs. Hesse and Ralph's wife (*Marilyn*) were here. I sewed quilt tops & bottom together.

Wed 9 – Very cloudy cool. Joseph came with the tractor and started to plow the pasture. We shelled corn and mixed feed.

Thurs 10 – 64 degrees, very foggy. Martin Armbruster was buried today. Geo went to the funeral. I went to church meeting at Columbia.

Fri 11 – Fair 69 in morning. I set up a quilt and started quilting.

Sat 12 – 64 degrees cloudy. Rained by afternoon, heavy at night.

Sun 13 – Rained mostly all day. Bill, Anita and June Ann were here. Went to Schilling's for Clara's birthday in the evening.

Mon 14 – Rained. I finished the quilt today and hemmed it too.

Tues 15 – Rain in morning, fair by noon. Josephs & Reinhardts were here. I cleaned up more in the granary shed.

Wed 16 – Very foggy 67 degrees. Josephs, Reinhardt and Geo & I were at St. Louis on business. Also stopped at Millstadt.

Thurs 17 – Rain by afternoon and most of the night. Mrs. Howerton came over and said they bought them a farm today.

Fri 18 – Very cloudy all day. We went to Belleville, Collinsville and Hecker with Roushes today. In evening I mixed feed.

Sat 19 – 62 degrees very foggy. I finished cleaning out the feed house.

Sun 20 – 58 degrees, fair. We were at Herman & Frank's then at Lang's for dinner. Home by 2:30 then Bill, Anita & June came. In evening we were at Hecker picnic. *Herman and Frank are Katie's bachelor brothers who live in a double log cabin on the Luetzelschwab homestead.*

Mon 21 – Fair 49 degrees. Patsy Glauber, Mrs. Roush and I were at the Home Bureau meeting at Mrs. T. L. Stookey's. Henry combined clover seed.

Tues 22 – 49 degrees, fair. I chopped weeds and cleaned around the summer house in the pasture. Henry combined more clover seed. Joseph started to plow.

Wed 23 – We worked about the place. Fair. Josephs mowed weeds and plowed.

Thurs 24 – Fair 59 degrees. I chopped weeds and worked about the place. We took spring chickens to Millstadt for 33 a lb.

Fri 25 – 66 degrees, partly cloudy. I worked about the yard. Was at Clara's a while in the afternoon.

Sat 26 – 69 degrees, fair. Howertons moved out today. Joseph's moved in. I went with Oscar & Elisa to visit Emma Barthel at the hospital.

Sun 27 – Rained, couldn't do much outdoors.

Mon 28 – Fair. I worked about the place. Also cooked grape jam and jelly.

Tues 29 – Fair, warm. We took chickens to Millstadt. Ramuald Schilling fixed our lights and Joseph's.

Wed 30 – We worked on the fence of the chicken yard and I dressed 4 chickens for the weekend.

Thurs 31 – We worked on the chicken yard fence today. Josephs helped us.

September 1950

Fri 1 – Irwin, Mary and children came in the afternoon. Rained a lot.

Sat 2 – Franklin, Gerry and the boys came back from their trip and spent the weekend with us. Rained hard towards evening. Bill, Anita & June came.

Sun 3 – We all were at Millstadt Homecoming. Then all the children spent the evening here at home with us. We had picture show.

Mon 4 – Irwin, Mary & children left for home this morning. Gerry & I washed. It was a nice cool day.

Tues 5 – Franklin and family & I were at Belleville, bought the quilt material then we had a wiener roast here for supper.

Wed 6 – Franklin & family left for Urbana this morning. Then I sewed the quilt tops and Alma marked one. Martha Mueth marked one.

Thurs 7 – Fair, very pretty day. We set up 2 quilts for the Grange and quilted afternoon & evening.

Fri 8 – Rain all day. We quilted on our Grange quilts, finished one.

Sat 9 – Rain all day. I went quilting at Floraville Grange. Finished one on Friday and then took the last one home today.

Sun 10 – Rainy to fair towards evening. Metzgers took us along to Broad Hollow Grange chicken supper. In evening Johnny, Katie & Mrs. Stepping were here.

Mon 11 – Fair after a heavy fog in morning. Johnny, Jakie, Henry Lang and Harold came and built our shed on the corn crib. Katie helped me. *John and Jacob "Jakie" Luetzelschwab are Katie's brothers. Henry Lang is her brother-in-law.*

Tues 12 – Fair, cooler. We worked about the place. Mrs. Mueth & Mrs. Kampe helped me hem quilt in evening.

Wed 13 – Partly cloudy, light shower early then fair. We were at Emerald Mound Grange in evening with Barthels. Pomona meeting.

Thurs 14 – Fair. We were at Millstadt, got 20.5 cents for hens. Helped Mrs. Roush quilt in afternoon. Went to the Grange meeting in evening.

Fri 15 – Fair to cloudy. I dressed 7 chickens for our Grange supper Sunday then I helped Mrs. Roush quilt. Orville Jung's were here in evening.

Sat 16 – Partly cloudy all day. We helped clean the Hall for our Grange chicken supper.

Sun 17 – Fair, very pretty day. Our picnic or Grange supper was good. Cleared $539. Janet's wedding was nice too.

Mon 18 – Fair, hot. We cleaned the church hall and then Mrs. Glauber & Mrs. Dennis came and we went to Daab's Clubhouse for Home Bureau.

Tues 19 – Fair hot. I worked about the place and ironed also made some apple sauce.

Wed 20 – Fair hot. Alma & I went along to Belleville to Christ Church dinner.

Thurs 21 – Rained hard shower in early morning. We cleaned out the chicken house. Went to the Grange Booster night in evening.

Fri 22 – Cloudy to fair. Mrs. Joseph and I went to Roush's for the quilting.

Sat 23 – Fair. I had quilts out airing and washed windows, put up new lace curtains in the east bedroom.

Sun 24 – 45 degrees. Stayed cold all day. Willie, Anita and June Ann came and we went to New Athens to visit Vera & Siegel Hesse. *Siegel was Anita's brother.*

Mon 25 – Fair cold 37 on our west porch. Stayed cold all day. We put tin siding on our new shed and then the men sowed fertilizer.

Tues 26 – Fair to cloudy. Henry Lang came to plow the sheep pasture. I stacked lumber for a while and canned apple sauce.

Wed 27 – Rainy all day so I worked indoors. Canned more apples.

Thurs 28 – Cloudy all day. Mrs. Joseph & I were quilting at Roush's. Irwin & Kenny came in the evening.

Fri 29 – Fair very warm. Irwin went to the Denmark Farms early this morning. He sold a carload of livestock to a Calif. man.

Sat 30 – Fair to cloudy. We worked about the place, also cleaned the chicken house. Irwin & Kenny left for home this morning.

October 1950

Sun 1 – Fair hot around 88 by noon. We spent the Sunday at home but went to Margret Probst's birthday in the evening.

Mon 2 – Fair hot. I washed and worked around outdoors for awhile. Geo made firewood.

Tues 3 – 62 degrees light rain during the night then turned colder. We worked with the lumber and firewood and I ironed some. Joseph started wheat sowing.

Wed 4 – 39 degrees. We made firewood and worked about the place.

Thurs 5 – 32 degrees for a short while not much frost damage yet. I went to Belleville St. Paul's Church meeting with Ida Gasser.

Fri 6 – 54 degrees cloudy south east winds, warmer. Mrs. Joseph helped me quilt. We were at the Guild meeting in the evening. Joseph is finished sowing wheat.

Sat 7 – Rain mostly all day. We were at Smithton to have our light fixed on the coupe. Henry & Harold were here. I quilted in the afternoon.

Sun 8 – Cloudy to rainy cold. We were at church in morning. The brothers Herman & Frank and Bill, Anita and June Ann came for the afternoon.

Mon 9 – Fair cold 41 degrees. Henry Lang started sowing wheat today. I quilted on Mrs. Roush's quilt.

Tues 10 – Fair cold around 45. We worked about the yard. I was in Belleville with Kleins.

Wed 11 – Cool fair. I stacked some lumber in the chicken yard. Mrs. Roush came in evening and we finished her quilt.

Thurs 12 – Fair getting very warm. Raymond and Geo & I picked the pears today. Had a pie contest at the Grange in evening.

Fri 13 – Cool. I baked rolls and mowed lawn. Langs finished sowing wheat yesterday.

Sat 14 – Hot 85 by afternoon. I mowed and raked the lawn and canned apple sauce and cleaned some.

Sun 15 – Fair. We stayed home all day. In evening we were at Lena Klein's birthday party.

Mon 16 – Fair. Ed & Alvina Feder were here all day. Roushes also stopped by awhile. Have to put up another quilt for tomorrow. *Ed Feder is George's first cousin on his mother's side who was a Feder.*

Tues 17 – Fair hot. We were at Millstadt, ordered $70 worth of cards from the Poehla Co. for the Home Ec Committee. Worked about the yard some.

Wed 18 – Fair hot around 87 to 90. Johnny & Jakie came and fixed up the corn crib. Katie quilted for me. We cleaned up the old boards.

Thurs 19 – Fair hot 85. Canned 3 qt apple sauce then Louis & Hattie came and stayed most of the day. Mrs. Joseph helped me quilt a while. *Louis Reiss is George's brother from Dallas, Texas.*

Fri 20 – Cooler, NW winds, fair very dry. Canned apple sauce. Geo shelled corn. Afternoon I worked about the yard.

Sat 21 – Fair 54 degrees. I canned more apple sauce and raked leaves and did my Saturday work.

Sun 22 – Cloudy all day. Willie, Anita and June Ann were here for dinner. Then Metzgers came and took us to wurstmarkt at Progressive Grange, then to Smithton Church.

Mon 23 – Cloudy and cold all day. We shelled corn and I also finished the quilt. John & Katie were here in the evening.

Tues 24 – 48 degrees, fair. I worked and then we cleaned out the corn crib. We were at the Paderborn card party with Metzgers.

Wed 25 – We were at Smithton, then I helped Josephs peel apples for apple butter. Geo finished shelling corn.

Thurs 26 – Josephs cooked apple butter. Franklin & George came and showed the pictures at the Grange. Mary & Lillian Weihl were here during the day. *Mary Weihl is Katie's sister. Lillian is her daughter.*

Fri 27 – Fair very warm. Geo & I went along home with Franklin to stay for the weekend. They took us to see the pep rally in town in evening.

Sat 28 – Fair warm. Mary and Irwin, Bill, Anita and June all came to Gerry & Franklin's house for dinner then went to the football game.

Sun 29 – Fair warm. We all went to Sunday School. Were in Franklin's class. Had dinner then left for home by one o'clock. Got to Hesse's at 5:30 PM.

Mon 30 – Fair hot and dry. We were tired so we went to Roush's in afternoon. Peeled apples in evening.

Tues 31 – Fair hot 85 by noon. We worked about the house and yard. Got the 135 cards today.

November 1950

Wed 1 – Fair hot winds turning to NW winds by evening with a few drops of rain, cooler. We had our Home Ec meeting here for the Xmas cards.

Thurs 2 – Cloudy and cold all day, 50. Metzgers took us along to the Broad Hollow Grange card party. Geo won a quilt.

Fri 3 – Cold cloudy 45 degrees. I mixed feed and carried in wood and put up the rest of the storm windows.

Sat 4 – 37 degrees stormy all day, getting colder. I did my Saturday work.

Sun 5 – 27 degrees, fair, everything is froze now. Edna, Henry and their children and girl and boyfriends were here for dinner. Ed & Lottie stopped in. Were at Gus Metzger's birthday in evening. *Edna Lang and Lottie Sander are Katie's sisters.*

Mon 6 – 40 degrees, fair. We worked about the place. Henry & Harold came with a load of wood and took the ventilator off the barn. Bill & Franklin came back from Texas.

Tues 7 – Rain all day, lightning and thunder. We sent the oil lease papers to Texas. Got my hair curled at Lottie Wiegand's. Voted and by evening it rained hard.

Wed 8 – Very cloudy 45. Roushes took us along to Belleville to the Farm Bureau meeting & dinner. Got very foggy by evening with a light drizzle.

Thurs 9 – Getting much colder by night. We were at the Grange meeting. We are all set to go to Belleville in the morning to take bus to Sullivan.

Fri 10 – Cloudy cold 22, snow flurries. Josephs took us to bus station, left for Indiana at 7:30 a.m. Arrived at Mary & Irwin's at 3:15 p.m.

Sat 11 – Fair, cold 18 above. Irwin, Mary and the children took us to Spring Mill State Park. Had a very nice trip of about 80 miles.

Sun 12 – Sunday. We all were at Sunday School.

Mon 13 – 30 degrees. Mary & Irwin went to Chicago at noon today and we stayed with the children.

Tues 14 – Fair to cloudy by evening. We stayed indoors mostly all day with the children.

Wed 15 – Rain all day. Mary & Irv came back by supper time, all fine.

Thurs 16 – Fair, warmer. We washed then I and the boys raked some leaves. Irwin worked the office.

Fri 17 – Mary the children and I drove out to buy a turkey for Saturday.

Sat 18 – Fair warm. We raked more leaves. Bill, Anita and June Ann came by afternoon. Had our Thanksgiving dinner in evening.

Sun 19 – Cloudy & rainy. We left for home at one o'clock noon. Got home at 6:30 p.m. Rained a lot during the night.

Mon 20 – Very stormy and much colder down to 25. We stayed indoors all day. I visited with Schillings a little while.

Tues 21 – Very cold 18 above, warmed up to about 40. I helped Josephs butcher a hog. Light drizzle at times.

Wed 22 – Fair and cloudy to colder by night. I washed. Irwin was operated on today. Mary called up at noon.

Thurs 23 – 37 degrees, very cloudy, getting much colder, snowed quite a bit. Mixed feed and carried in wood. 2 inch of snow on ground. Went to Grange meeting.

Fri 24 – 9 above, warmer towards evening. I worked about the place.

Sat 25 – Slightly warmer, colder by night. I did my Saturday work.

Sun 26 – Fair, stormy cold, warmed up by evening. So we went to church for a picture show. Called Irwin & Mary to know how Irwin was.

Mon 27 – Somewhat warmer. I worked in the house, also mixed feed.

Tues 28 – Fair to cloudy, very cold wind 22 degrees. Metzgers & I went to Hecker for Ted Klein's wedding. Then we went to Belleville. Went to wedding dance in evening.

Wed 29 – Still cold. Mrs. Roush came and we set up a quilt. Ground is frozen hard.

Thurs 30 – Fair, not so cold. I mixed feed. In evening Mrs. Kampe got me to go to Martha's for our meeting.

December 1950

Fri 1 – Very cloudy warmer. Josephs sawed firewood for us. In the evening we went home with Willie and the Hunters. June had a birthday.

Sat 2 – Very warm 60 by noon. We prepared for June's birthday celebration. It rained hard by evening and turned colder.

Sun 3 – Fair very pretty day. Hesses came to Willie & Anita's for the day. We had a 20 lb turkey. Hesses took us home in evening.

Mon 4 – Cold. I mixed feed and went to Columbia with Josephs. Hauled in a lot of wood and coal.

Tues 5 – Rain turned to snow. I was to a quilting at Schilling's. Snow slowly all day.

Wed 6 – Very cold 9 above. Didn't get over 15 all day. Still snowing and blowing drifts. I quilted.

Thurs 7 – Partly cloudy very cold around zero. Didn't get above 14 all day. I quilted again.

Fri 8 – 15 above, fair, warmed up to 32, colder again by night. Metzgers took us along to Floraville Guild Xmas gift exchange and program.

Sat 9 – 20 above, fair much warmer but wind turned to NW again. I quilted then we hauled in firewood and did some Saturday work.

Sun 10 – Fair, cold. Bill and his boss were here hunting.

Mon 11 – Fair cold. I worked about the house and brought in firewood.

Tues 12 – Cold. I washed and ironed and did my house work.

Wed 13 – Fair cold, couldn't do any outdoors work.

Thurs 14 – I baked cookies and worked about the house. Were at the Grange meeting in the evening.

Fri 15 – Fair. I baked cookies and mixed feed.

Sat 16 – Cold. I mixed feed and did my Saturday work.

Sun 17 – Fair, cold, didn't get above 16 all day. Herman & Frank were here for dinner. Were at our Grange potluck & Xmas party in the evening.

Mon 18 – Fair, 15 above. Patsy took me along to Seibert's for the Christmas potluck dinner & Home Bureau meeting. In evening we were at Turkey Hill Grange with Metzgers.

Tues 19 – Fair, cold 12 above. I baked cookies today.

Wed 20 – Fair, cold 10 above in morning. Gus & Alma took us to Broad Hollow Grange in evening. Officers' installation. Afternoon we were at oil meeting in Belleville with Roushes.

Thurs 21 – Cloudy to fair, 20 degrees warmed up to 35. Mr. Joseph & I were butchering at Elsie & Albert's.

Fri 22 – Fair getting warmer. I cleaned the beds and the rooms.

Sat 23 – Fair, very pretty and warm. Irwin & Mary and children came by 3 o'clock. We had a nice evening together.

Sun 24 – Fair, very pretty day. We all were at Bill & Anita's for dinner & supper. Franklin came there by 3 o'clock. Uncle Will also was there.

Mon 25 – Fair, very warm 40 degrees. We all opened our Christmas packages and had a lovely day together. All the children were home for supper.

Tues 26 – Very stormy, snow flurries. The children all left for their homes again. Cleaned up by noon. In evening Geo & I were at Elisa Koerber's birthday.

Wed 27 – Fair, cold 8 above. Ramuald Schilling and I were at Elmer Probst's for awhile. Their house burned some. Then I went to Mrs. Roush's. She sewed the quilt tops.

Thurs 28 – 20 degrees, warmed up by noon. I cleaned and aired bed things. Were at Grange meeting in evening.

Fri 29 – Fair 22 degrees. I helped Joseph butcher. In evening Alma & Lena Klein helped me mark the card party quilt. Saturday we were at Henry & Edna's.

Sat 30 – Fair 22 degrees, warmed up much by noon.

Sun 31 – 25 degrees, fair strong south winds. We had company most of the day. In evening we were at Schilling's.

1951

January 1951

Mon 1 – 37 degrees, very cloudy, rain slowly all day. We were at church then John & Katie came for dinner. We played cards in afternoon.

Tues 2 – Rainy all day, strong south winds, 45 degrees. I set up the card party quilt.

Wed 3 – Fair to cloudy. I was at Belleville with Schillings to make out income report. Had quilting in evening.

Thurs 4 – Fair, warm, no frost. I had quilting for the card party. Roads very muddy.

Fri 5 – Fair, warm, 50 degrees. We were to the Guild meeting in evening. We were at Waterloo in morning to visit Mary & Lillian. I paid women's Guild dues for 1951.

Sat 6 – Very cloudy turning much colder, snowed lightly by night. Metzgers took us along to Robert Probst's birthday party.

Sun 7 – Fair 10 above. We stayed home all day. Had come & go company all day.

Mon 8 – 15 above, fair. We got our storm windows today. I quilted.

Tues 9 – Fair, warmer. I quilted. Geo did the feeding.

Wed 10 – Fair. I quilted all day. Roads are awful muddy. We want to saw wood tomorrow.

Thurs 11 – Fair to cloudy. I quilted. Were at Grange meeting in evening. We cashed our oil check today.

Fri 12 – Cloudy not cold, no frost, very muddy. I quilted or set up the baby quilt which Anita sent for me to quilt. In evening we quilted at Schilling's.

Sat 13 – Cloudy and rainy. I quilted on Anita's baby quilt. Willie called in evening and said Anita has a bad cold and that they couldn't come Sunday.

Sun 14 – Rainy all day & snow flurries. We stayed home all day. I quilted. In evening we played cards at Joseph's.

Mon 15 – Rain turning to snow but melted as it fell, clearing by night, colder. I quilted all day. I mailed the baby quilt to Anita today.

Tues 16 – Fair 27 degrees white frost, south winds. I finished the card party quilt today.

Wed 17 – Very pretty day, warm. We were at our Grange card party, had a good crowd. I worked in the cake & coffee stand.

Thurs 18 – Fair, very pretty day, no frost, 69 by noon. We helped clean the hall. Then I washed and ironed yet.

Fri 19 – Very foggy in morning, then fair & warm, 70 by 2 p.m. We took chickens to Smithton. Then I mixed feed and worked in the house.

Sat 20 – Warm, 62 degrees turning colder, very stormy, 33 degrees by 4 o'clock, 30 by night. I did my Saturday work. Took down the Christmas tree.

Sun 21 – Sunday, 14 above, fair 22 degrees by noon. We stayed home all day.

Mon 22 – Cold south winds. We started to clean the chicken house and I also cleaned up the basement.

Tues 23 – Fair, no frost in ground but got colder by night. I helped quilt at Marcella's afternoon & evening.

Wed 24 – We cleaned the chicken house today. Ludger Schilling came home for his first furlough. We got a 2 dollar Waterloo Milk Co. check.

Thurs 25 – Fair, much colder around 22 at noon. I baked a silver wedding cake for Mr. & Mrs. Frank Klein. We celebrated at the Grange in the evening. Had a nice evening.

Fri 26 – Fair to cloudy, no frost. We cleaned the brooder house and took wood in the basement. Were at Schilling's in evening to see Ludger.

Sat 27 – Cloudy, getting much colder. I carried in a lot of wood & coal and put litter into the chicken house and swept the basement.

Sun 28 – Rain snow flurries & sleet, not much tho, made slick ice. This was Sunday but we stayed home. Getting very cold 15 above by evening.

Mon 29 – Cloudy, 3 below. Didn't get above 12 all day. I quilted. Geo did the feeding as I have a cold. I set up Mrs. Hulet's quilt and started quilting. *Mrs. Hulet is Gerry Reiss' mother in Urbana, Illinois.*

Tues 30 – 3 below at St. Louis, 1 below here, didn't get above 12 all day, partly cloudy. I quilted, Geo did the feeding.

Wed 31 – 8 above zero, started snowing by eleven o'clock and kept it up all day, never got above 11 all day. I quilted. Geo did the feeding. Strong NW winds.

February 1951

Thurs 1 – 4 below zero, clearing, did not get above 8 all day, 5 below by 8 o'clock p.m., 8 below by midnight. I stayed up till 1:30 to keep the fire going.

Fri 2 – 10 below zero on our front porch at 8 o'clock in morning, 13 below at Millstadt at 5 o'clock morning, still 5 below at 9 in morning.

Sat 3 – 10 above, fair to cloudy, some snow by night. I cleaned up for Sunday.

Sun 4 – 21 above, fair. The Roush boys gave Bill, Anita & June a sleigh ride with their horses & sleigh, also a horseback ride.

Mon 5 – Fair, nice day 22 above. Joseph's butchered a hog for us. Started to rain by night.

Tues 6 – Rained all day, clearing by night, wind turned to NW, got much colder, creeks were out. Irwin came and we went to Millstadt for his program.

Wed 7 – Fair, 10 above, strong NW winds all day. Irwin left for Texas at noon. Schillings & Marcella were here to help me quilt.

Thurs 8 – Snowed lightly all day, 18 degrees. Mrs. Fred Wachtel helped me quilt. In evening we were at the Grange meeting.

Fri 9 – Cloudy, cold 15 above. I quilted all day.

Sat 10 – 20 degrees, fair, windy from the south. I finished Mrs. Hulet's quilt and mixed feed. Geo shelled and crushed corn. Joseph brought us wood.

Sun 11 – Fair, windy from the south, 40 degrees. We were at church. Then I baked some pies. Irwin came back from Texas yesterday noon and left for home.

Mon 12 – Warm, 56 in early morning, very muddy. Joseph's butchered and made summer sausage. I fried down our pork sausage.

Tues 13 – Rained, turned colder by night around 42 degrees all day. I set up Mrs. Kruppa's quilt.

Wed 14 – 24 degrees, sleeting all day. I quilted all day. Geo was reading and sleeping.

Thurs 15 – 30 degrees, getting warmer, rained all day & night. Josephs took us to the Woodman card party at Floraville.

Fri 16 – 38 degrees, cloudy, rained all last night. I'm frying down bacon today.

Sat 17 – 42 degrees, warmed up to 57 by noon, very pretty day but awful muddy. Geo crushed corn. I mixed feed.

Sun 18 – 45 degrees, warmed up to 60 by afternoon. Rained all morning. We were at Joseph's to celebrate Mrs. Joseph's birthday.

Mon 19 – 52 degrees, foggy, cloudy, rain by night. I quilted. Geo was reading, couldn't do any outdoors work.

Tues 20 – 54 degrees. Rained hard mostly all day, wind turned to NW by night and got very strong. I quilted.

Wed 21 – 37 degrees, still very cloudy. Alma & I were quilting at Floraville. In the evening I finished Mrs. Kruppa's quilt.

Thurs 22 – 40 degrees, mostly cloudy. Irwin came towards evening and stayed overnight. We were at the Grange meeting. Frost during the night.

Fri 23 – 30 degrees, fair, warmed up to 54. Got our chicks today. Irwin left for home by 9:30 a.m. Afternoon Josephs & we sawed wood.

Sat 24 – Partly cloudy 47 degrees, 52 by noon. I did my Saturday work.

Sun 25 – Warm 50 degrees. We were to our church potluck supper in the evening. Were at church in morning.

Mon 26 – Cloudy to fair, no frost. I washed and worked about the place, pruned some grapes.

Tues 27 – Shower during night, fair warm during day. We were at Schilling's & Roush's to collect for new hospital.

Wed 28 – Rained during the night, very cloudy all day. We got feed at Smithton & signed up for AAA program. Was to a quilting at Schilling's in afternoon.

March 1951

Thurs 1 – Fair cooler around 32, warmed up by noon to 52, rained by night, windy all day. I finished pruning grapes.

Fri 2 – Rainy in morning. I worked and cleaned in the house. Also patched and darned socks. Geo & Josephs were to a meeting in evening at Waterloo.

Sat 3 – No frost, cloudy to fair after a shower in morning, 66 degrees. I patched. Bill, Anita & June Ann were here for supper in evening.

Sun 4 – Fair, 32 degrees, light frost. I was to a Stanley Party at Mrs. Arthur Mehrmann's.

Mon 5 – 35 degrees, warmed up to 59, windy from SE, cloudy. I had a cold so I stayed indoors and darned socks.

Tues 6 – 52 degrees in morning, 74 by afternoon. Partly cloudy. Geo & I took 14 hens to Millstadt, got 29 a lb.

Wed 7 – Cooler, 35 in morning. I worked about the place. In the evening we were at church.

Thurs 8 – Fair getting colder, 57 at noon. We were at Grange meeting in evening. Raymond took us up.

Fri 9 – Cold 23 in morning, ground froze hard. Langs sowed their clover seed today. Geo shelled corn. I cleaned some in the brooder shed.

Sat 10 – Rain all day 33 degrees, first rain was freezing, turned warmer later in the day. I did my Saturday work.

Sun 11 – 35 degrees, rained all day, no hard rain tho. We stayed home all day. Played cards at Joseph's in evening.

Mon 12 – 35 degrees, still drizzling. I worked about the house. Started snowing towards evening. John Rapps were here.

Tues 13 – 23 degrees, still snowing lightly about 2 inches. Snowed all day. I sewed & patched all day.

Wed 14 – 30 degrees, strong northwest winds with snow flurries all day. I darned socks for Rapps.

Thurs 15 – 30 degrees, strong northwest winds. I'll patch Rapp's overalls today.

Fri 16 – 22 degrees, fair, 4 in snow, warmed up to 40 by noon. I sewed & patched. Snow melted.

Sat 17 – 38 degrees, rained hard at night, thundershowers. I did my Saturday work.

Sun 18 – Fair 35 degrees strong northwest winds. We were at church then stayed home. Roush boys were here a while.

Mon 19 – 21 degrees strong northwest winds. Roushes and I were at the Home Bureau meeting at Marjorie Skaer's.

Tues 20 – Fair, cold 21 above. We let our chicks out into the shed for the first time. I went to the quilting for the Woodmen in the evening with Koerbers.

Wed 21 – 13 above, 4 inches snow fell through the night, most of it melted today as it warmed up to 40 by afternoon. We cleaned the brooder house.

Thurs 22 – 25 degrees, strong south winds. We took hens & eggs to Millstadt, got 34 cents a lb for hens, 38 eggs. We were at the Grange meeting.

Fri 23 – Fair cold 27 degrees, warmed up to 40. Irwin & Mary and the children came last night. Irwin went to the south farms today.

Sat 24 – Fair 33 degrees. Irwin came back this morning, then Irv & Mary & Mary Kay went to East St. Louis. Franklin & family came by noon.

Sun 25 – Fair, very pretty 35 degrees, warmed up nicely. We all went to church and all the children went to communion with me on my 61st birthday. Geo didn't feel good so he stayed home.

Mon 26 – White frost 32 degrees, fair to partly cloudy. Irwin & Franklin & families left for home today. Afternoon Clara & Allie came. Birthday club in evening.

Tues 27 – Cloudy, light showers. I worked about the yard and also cleaned up in the house. Geo made some firewood.

Wed 28 – Showery, 57 degrees, cloudy with light showers thru the day. I planted some tulip bulbs. Metzgers & we were at Smithton in evening.

Thurs 29 – Rain all day, mostly afternoon. We cleaned the brooder house in the morning. We & Reinhardts were playing cards at Joseph's in the evening.

Fri 30 – Cold 36 degrees, snow flurries, then fair but stormy till evening. Metzgers took us along to Turkey Hill Grange to see the degree work.

Sat 31 – Fair 32 degrees, white frost then very pretty day, warmed up nicely. I washed, also bedspreads. Geo cut firewood.

April 1951

Sun 1 – Partly cloudy, 36 degrees, northwest winds. I set up a quilt.

Mon 2 – Cold NW winds 34 in the morning, 40 by noon. I quilted.

Tues 3 – Fair cold NW winds. We cleaned the brooder house. Then I quilted awhile.

Wed 4 – Fair nice day around 50 by noon. We got the canna bulbs at Roush's and I worked about the yard. Josephs sowed oats today.

Thurs 5 – Partly cloudy, cold east wind all day. We were at Hesse's in the afternoon, also got some chick feed at Smithton.

Fri 6 – Warmer 50 in morning, 60 late, thundershowers throughout the day. I had a bad cold so I couldn't work very much.

Sat 7 – 32 degrees, white frost, showery cold winds all day. I quilted. I had a cold so didn't go out much.

Sun 8 – 34 degrees, rainy at times through the day. Herman & Frank were here in the afternoon. In evening we played cards at Joseph's. *Herman and Frank Luetzelschwab are Katie's brothers.*

Mon 9 – Fair to cloudy with sleet & rain at times, 34 degrees in morning, warmed up to 50. We cleaned the brooder house.

Tues 10 – 40 degrees, fair, warmed up to 60. I was at Spring Festival at Millstadt church. Josephs built the yard fence today.

Wed 11 – 38 degrees, rained all day. Geo & I were to the Pomona Grange meeting at Floraville in the evening. I quilted during the day.

Thurs 12 – 34 degrees, snow flurries mostly all day, cleared in evening. We both & Raymond were at the Grange meeting. Raymond got his first & second degrees. *Raymond Joseph is the son of the Reiss farm tenants and lives in the older home with his parents.*

Fri 13 – 39 degrees, rained all day and night. I quilted.

Sat 14 – 42 degrees, fair, very pretty day, warmed up to 70 by noon. We cleaned the brooder house. Geo made firewood. I did my Saturday work.

Sun 15 – 41 degrees, northwest wind, partly cloudy all day. Bill, Anita and June Ann were here.

Mon 16 – Fair, cold, windy. Mrs. Glauber, Mrs. Dennis & I were at the Home Bureau meeting at Mrs. F. Knipping's.

Tues 17 – Fair, very pretty all after a heavy frost in morning, 31 degrees, warmed up to 55. Mrs. Roush helped me finish the quilt.

Wed 18 – 50 degrees, warmed up to 70 by afternoon showers and cooler by night. I planted my first cannas today.

Thurs 19 – 40 degrees, warmed up to 65 by noon. I planted geraniums. We were at Millstadt, got 40 cents for eggs and 30 for hens.

Fri 20 – Partly cloudy around 50 degrees. I planted more cannas. We cleaned the brooder house. Irwin, Mary and the children came in the evening.

Sat 21 – Rained just about all day long. Mary & Irwin & Bill, Anita and June were at St. Louis to visit Henry & Bertha.

Sun 22 – Fair but cold and windy. The Hesse family and Ralph & Marilyn and baby (*Carolyn*) & Bill, Anita, June and Uncle Will all were here for Pop's birthday.

Mon 23 – Fair, white frost, but warmed up nicely. Birthday club was here last night. The men built us a new telephone line in here from Klein's.

Tues 24 – Fair warmer, 50 in morning. Geo & I were at Belleville. I had to take a lesson for the Home Bureau.

Wed 25 – Partly cloudy to fair, 84 degrees by noon. I cooked for the wedding at Mueth's.

Thurs 26 – Fair, warm 80 degrees by noon. The Grange members celebrated our 40th wedding anniversary this evening.

Fri 27 – Fair, warm around 82 by noon. I worked about the yard. Had our pie social at the Grange in the evening.

Sat 28 – 79 degrees at 7:30 a.m., got up to 86 by noon. Got feed at Smithton. I dressed 3 chickens. Were at Mrs. Joseph's birthday in evening.

Sun 29 – Fair very hot, 79 in morning. We were at Walter Brandenburger's in afternoon.

Mon 30 – Fair hot 75 in morning, got up to 87 by afternoon. I worked in the garden. We got a new battery for the coupe today from Reinhardt.

May 1951

Tues 1 – Fair to cloudy, hot 85. We had the truck tested and took eggs & chickens to Millstadt. I helped Mrs. Fred Wachtel quilt in afternoon.

Wed 2 – Fair, hot today but rained last night, nice slow rain which helped a lot. I planted tomatoes today, also glad bulbs & flowers.

Thurs 3 – 54 degrees, fair to cloudy, much warmer by noon. We worked about the place.

Fri 4 – Cloudy showers by night. I gave the program this evening for the women's guild. Cool around 60 degrees. Joseph planted corn.

Sat 5 – 55 degrees. I spaded and planted flowers. Mary & Lillian were here for dinner. We had some feed crushed in the morning. *Mary Weihl is Katie's sister and Lillian is Mary's daughter.*

Sun 6 – Cold 53 degrees. We went to church. Katie Petry was here a while. We & Metzgers took us along to Dara Mueth's. *Katie Petry is George's sister.*

Mon 7 – 54 degrees, fair. I planted more flowers. Roush got 12 chickens today.

Tues 8 – 60 degrees, fair & warmer. I worked about the yard & garden.

Wed 9 – Partly cloudy 60 degrees. I planted more dahlias and was at County Home Bureau meeting at Millstadt at Bluff Pomona meeting in evening.

Thurs 10 – 65 degrees, raining slow for several hours. We were at the Grange meeting in the evening.

Fri 11 – Fair cold winds, 50. Orlin Skaer painted the living room first coat.

Sat 12 – Fair warmer. I cut the lawn and planted some dahlias & cannas. We were to a birthday party at Glassmaker's.

Sun 13 – Cool all day. Bill, Anita and June were here for dinner. Then we all went to Hesse's. Irwin called up for Mothers Day.

Mon 14 – Fair 80 degrees. I finished spading & planting the front yard flower bed then hoed a lot of weeds.

Tues 15 – Fair, hot, got up to 90. It's awful dry. I hoed weeds and planted more cannas.

Wed 16 – 69 degrees. Orlin finished painting the living room. Irwin came by 4 o'clock. Bill, Anita & June came & we all had supper together.

Thurs 17 – 84 degrees in morning, 90 by 3 p.m. Irwin went to the south farms this morning. I worked about the yard and house.

Fri 18 – 76 degrees in morning. I finished planting cannas & dahlias and hoed weeds and dressed 4 chickens. 92 degrees by 3 p.m.

Sat 19 – 80 degrees in morning, 90 by noon. I picked the first strawberries in orchard today. Baked rolls & a cake, did Saturday work.

Sun 20 – Fair shower during night. Henry & Bertha (*Reiss*), Carlena & Elmer (*Gummersheimer*), Orville & Helen (*Koerber*) & Janet Jung and Lizzie Buechle were here for dinner.

Mon 21 – Fair to cloudy, rain by night. We were at Roush's for the Home Bureau meeting. I gave major lesson.

Tues 22 – Rained off and on night and day. We left for Indiana at 5 o'clock in morning, got home by 10 in evening.

Wed 23 – Cool 57 degrees, rained during night, but fair in day. We cleaned the brooder house.

Thurs 24 – Fair cool 58 degrees. We started cleaning hen house, cut some of the lawn, were at Grange meeting.

Fri 25 – Fair 64 degrees. We cleaned the hen house. I planted butter beans and cut the lawn. Joseph planted corn in bottoms.

Sat 26 – 68 degrees at 7 in morning, shower during the night.

Sun 27 – Fair, hot 87 degrees.

Mon 28 – Fair. We were at Kampe's and Steiffler's to see about the strawberries for Grange social. I washed in the afternoon.

Tues 29 – Showers to fair. We were at Millstadt. Loretta Joseph gave me a Toni. *Toni was a brand name of a hair permanent.*

Wed 30 – Fair, hot. We were at Smithton for the Memorial Day program. I ironed in the morning.

Thurs 31 – We had a nice slow rain in the morning, afternoon fair. I planted more lima beans.

Photographs

I owe special thanks also to the late Franklin Reiss, Katie's middle son, who took all the photographs in this book.

Aerial photo of Reiss Family Farm showing year various parcels were purchased.
#1 is the log cabin built in 1834 and used by the Adam Reiss and then the Frank
Reiss families until 1889. #2 is a log cabin used from 1866 to 1889 by the widow
of Adam Reiss and her second husband Conrad Ebert. #3 is a modern house built
in 1889 by Frank Reiss and later used by George and Katie Reiss. #4 is a modern
house built in 1941 by George and Katie Reiss. #5 is the farmstead of Marcella
and "Boobie" Klein. #6 is the farmstead of Clara and Frank Shilling who were
Marcella's parents. #7 is the Smithton Sportsmans Club.

Katie and George Reiss from about 1935

Kaite and George Reiss

Kaite and George Reiss

Grandparents and grandchildren. From left are George, June Ann, George, Richard, Steve, Ken, Mary Kay, and Katie.

The extended Katie and George Reiss family. Back row from left is Gerry, George, June Ann, Bill, Mary, Katie, Anita, and Irv. Front row from left is Mary Kay, George, Richard, Steve, and Ken

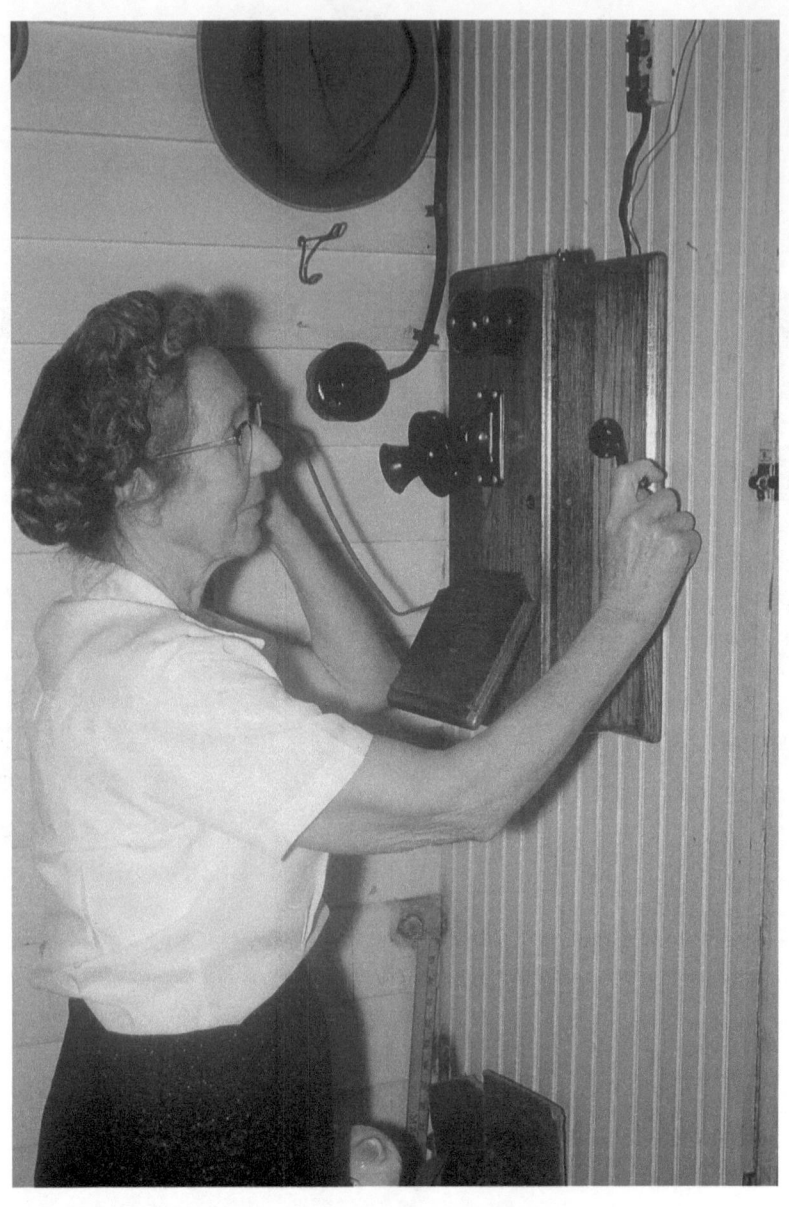

Katie at private wall telephone line to Schillings and Kleins

Log cabin built by Adam Reiss in 1834

Log cabin built by Adam Reiss in 1834 and modern house built by Frank Reiss in 1889

Modern house built by Frank Reiss in 1889

Foreground is log barn built by Adam Reiss in 1834 and background is conventional barn built by George Reiss about 1920.

Modern house built by Katie and George Reiss in 1941

Woods road looking toward the homestead.

Woods road looking toward the mailbox.

Smithton Sportsmens Club, Lake #1

Smithton Sportsmens Club, ice skating on lake #1

St. Paul United Church of Christ in Floraville where all three sons of Katie and George were confirmed

One room school in Floraville attended by all three sons of Katie and George

June 1951

Fri 1 – Fair hot. We finished cleaning the hen house and cut weeds about the place.

Sat 2 – Fair to cloudy, very hot 93 degrees, thunderstorm and very heavy rain by evening, rained at
least 6 inches in 2 hours.

Sun 3 – Very cloudy, rainy by night. We had our strawberry social today. Used 3.5 trays at $3.25 a tray from Steiffler's.

Mon 4 – Cloudy, cold 56 degrees. We cleaned the church hall and went voting. Then I marked Gerry's quilt.

Tues 5 – Fair 52 degrees. I cut weeds and hoed in the garden. In evening were at Weigand's silver wedding anniversary at Smithton.

Wed 6 – Fair to partly cloudy. We Guild ladies were at Waterloo for a Guild meeting.

Thurs 7 – Rained some. Mary & Irwin and the children came towards evening. Very cool.

Fri 8 – Fair to cloudy and a bad storm and hard rain by night. Irwin was at the south farms. Mary & I set up Gerry's quilt.

Sat 9 – Fair. We sewed on the quilt and Mary made a dress for Mary Kay. Irwin came back by noon.

Sun 10 – Fair cool. We all went to Hesse's for the wedding anniversary. Had a picnic dinner in the lawn.

Mon 11 – Fair very pretty day. I cut weeds and washed. Mrs. Roush came to help me quilt. Children were at the zoo.

Tues 12 – Rained thru the night. Mary & Irwin left for Canton farm. The children are staying with us. Stevie's birthday today.

Wed 13 – Rained hard thru the night. I quilted and took care of the children.

Thurs 14 – 65 degrees, partly cloudy. I cut some weeds and quilted and washed some things. We took our 3 grandchildren to Grange meeting.

Fri 15 – Fair but had rained hard during the night. Irwin & Mary came back today. The children were glad.

Sat 16 – Cloudy with some rain. We all went to Fort Chartres had our dinner along and had a nice time.

Sun 17 – Fair. We all went to John & Katie's and found that Katie had gone to the hospital so we went there too to see her. Also took in the Smithton picnic.

Mon 18 – Irwin went to work and at the Denmark farm. I was to the Home Bureau meeting. Canned cherries in the evening.

Tues 19 – We canned gooseberries, made 8 pints for Mary and 4 pints for me but I have some more to can. Visited Klein's towards evening. Rained hard in the night.

Wed 20 – It rained several times during the day. Irwin came back from the Denmark farm. I baked a cake and hemmed the quilt. Mary took care of the children.

Thurs 21 – Cloudy and showery. Joseph took a load of wheat to Columbia, got $1.97 a bu. Then we cleaned out the granary. Irwin, Mary, and children left for home.

Fri 22 – Cloudy light shower by afternoon. We got oats ground at Smithton then I transplanted some flowers.

Sat 23 – Very cloudy and cool all day, a shower by 4 p.m. We were visiting with Herman & Frank and Langs. Then we dressed 2 chickens.

Sun 24 – 72 degrees in early morning.

Mon 25 – 68 degrees, hot by noon. We picked the first dewberries also canned cherries. Rained hard by 6 p.m.

Tues 26 – 68 degrees in morning, rained all morning, fair & hot afternoon. Metzgers and I were at Belleville to see Katie at hospital.

Wed 27 – Hot in early morning 80 degrees, thundershowers by afternoon. We picked dewberries. Then visited at Schilling's.

Thurs 28 – Rainy in morning, very cloudy all day. I baked pies then we visited Schillings awhile. Grange meeting in evening.

Fri 29 – Rain in early morning. We picked 1.5 gal dewberries. Rapps came and picked cherries. We dressed some chickens in evening.

Sat 30 – We picked dewberries and canned green beans. We & Metzgers were at Mehrmann's wedding.

July 1951

Sun 1 – Fair pretty day. We were at church, then Ed and Lena came stayed for supper.

Mon 2 – Fair very pretty day. I washed a big wash and ironed some and got things ready to go to Urbana.

Tues 3 – Fair hot. Langs & Josephs combined wheat today. We picked dewberries, also took berries & chicken to locker.

Wed 4 – Fair very pretty day. We left for Urbana at 5 a.m. got there at 9:15. We had a nice visit with Franklin & Gerry & boys.

Thurs 5 – Rainy all day. We and Rapps came back from Urbana at 1:15 noon. I ironed some in the evening.

Fri 6 – Pretty cloudy and very cool. Marcella & I went to see the airplane which crashed in Schilling's pasture this morning.

Sat 7 – Fair hot 88 to 90. Langs combined wheat. I mowed lawn and baked and dressed chicken.

Sun 8 – Fair very hot 90 degrees. We were at Roush's in afternoon otherwise we didn't do much as it was Sunday.

Mon 9 – Hard rain in early morning. I canned beans and mixed feed and darned socks.

Tues 10 – Rained in morning. Then we went to Smithton to pay our 1950 taxes. It was $417.14. Afternoon I patched.

Wed 11 – Rain thru the night and early morning. Afternoon we both pulled weeds.

Thurs 12 – Rained in morning. We pulled weeds afternoon. Were to the Grange meeting in evening.

Fri 13 – Raining hard. I set up Mrs. Kruppa's quilt. Quit raining by noon and cleared up.

Sat 14 – Fair hot around 90 by noon. Langs combined a few hoppers full but got stuck in low places. Geo & I were at Rist's sale.

Sun 15 – Fair not quite so hot but around 88. We were at church then the hunting club came. Then Franklin & family came. Langs finished combining.

Mon 16 – Fair hot. Franklin & Gerry and boys & I were at Belleville to meet with the Sportsman's Club & Otis Guyman lawyer.

Tues 17 – Fair hot. Franklin, Gerry, George, Richard, June Ann and I were on the boat excursion. In evening the Sportsman Club and Bill & Franklin met here. *This is the initial meeting between the Smithton Sportsmen's Club and the extended Reiss family to discuss a long term lease of 40 acres on the east edge of the Reiss Farm where the Sportsmen's would eventually build three lakes and a clubhouse for their meetings and recreation.*

Wed 18 – Fair hot. Franklin, Gerry and boys left for home. Then I cleaned up the kitchen, also quilted awhile.

Thurs 19 – Fair hot. I washed today and pulled weeds in evening. Canned apple sauce.

Fri 20 – Fair hot. I quilted and weeded the flowers.

Sat 21 – Fair hot. I worked about the house and yard. We were at the Paderborn picnic in evening with Metzgers.

Sun 22 – Fair very hot. Bill, Anita and June Ann came in afternoon. We had a hard rain in evening.

Mon 23 – Fair hot. I quilted and canned apple sauce. Josephs finished combining oats, about 180 in all. Our share 60 bu.

Tues 24 – Fair hot. We were at Schilling's awhile. Joseph's horse got hurt in the private telephone line wire. Irwin came in evening.

Wed 25 – Very foggy and cloudy. Irwin left for home this morning. We gathered apples and I quilted.

Thurs 26 – 87 in early morning. Hot thru out the day. Mrs. Roush helped me quilt. We were at Grange meeting in evening.

Fri 27 – Fair hot in the 90s by afternoon, thundering by evening, not much rain tho. I weeded in the yard and quilted & canned pickles.

Sat 28 – Fair very hot 93 by noon. I cut lawn, pulled weeds and quilted. Metzgers took us along to see the Smithton parade.

Sun 29 – Cooler. We were in church then we rested and in the evening we went to the Smithton picnic with Metzgers.

Mon 30 – Cool in early morning. I wrote letters first then worked about the yard. Mr. Robert Ehret and Mr. Jacob Leiner paid 20 dollars for hunting on Schaefer farm only.

Tues 31 – Rained hard for a while, then fair. I worked about the yard and quilted at times. Had committee meeting here for our picnic.

August 1951

Wed 1 – Fair not so hot. We and Metzgers were at the fair all day. In evening I quilted.

Thurs 2 – Fair hot. Alvina Rapp and I were at Belleville to buy prizes for our Grange picnic. Towards evening I cut lawn.

Fri 3 – Cloudy to fair, hot. Harold and Myrtle hauled a load of wheat for us, got $1.99 a bu. Alma & I marked a quilt for the Grange picnic.

Sat 4 – Fair cooler. I cut the lawn and picked blackberries and sewed quilt tops and bottoms together.

Sun 5 – Very cool 60 degrees, fair. We were at the Woodman picnic at Floraville.

Mon 6 – Light rain in morning, fair & warmer or rather hot by afternoon. Alma & I marked another quilt.

Tues 7 – Hot & humid, cloudy. I quilted and chopped weeds. Geo chopped weeds too. Josephs hauled wheat today, got $2.00 a bu.

Wed 8 – Fair hot. Alvina and I set up 2 quilts for the Grange today and we quilted till evening. *Alvina Feder is George's first cousin.*

Thurs 9 – I went to Floraville at noon to help quilt and I stayed for evening as it was Grange meeting. Juvenile Grange was organized.

Fri 10 – I cut lawn and cleaned about the place. Mary & Irwin came late at night. We had a shower today.

Sat 11 – Fair not quite so hot. I only did my house work.

Sun 12 – Fair. Bill & Anita were here to visit with Irv & Mary. Afternoon Bill, Irwin, Pop, Steven, Kenny and I all went to see our land below Paderborn.

Mon 13 – Fair. Irwin & Mary left for Springfield to go to the fair, then to Canton, Ill. The children are here with us.

Tues 14 – Fair hot. Vera Hesse brought June Ann today to stay with us for the week. *Vera is June Ann's aunt or the wife of Anita's brother Siegel Hesse.*

Wed 15 – Had a shower today. June & I baked cookies also washed the clothes. Irwin & Mary came back late evening.

Thurs 16 – Mary & I visited with each other this morning. Irv went to St. Louis. I went quilting.

Fri 17 – Fair not quite so hot. We had a wiener roast in the evening, after Franklin and family got here.

Sat 18 – Franklin, Gerry & I gathered ground samples this morning to have it tested. The men started on the lake today.

Sun 19 – Bill, Anita, Franklin and Gerry, Irwin & Mary, all went on the boat last night. I kept the children.

Mon 20 – The children were all home with us yesterday. Irwin & Mary left for home in the afternoon. Franklin & family left today.

Tues 21 – Rained last night. Got quite cool today. I washed and ironed some too.

Wed 22 – Very cool 63 degrees in morning. I aired some clothes today and went quilting in afternoon.

Thurs 23 – Very cool 62 degrees. I baked bread & rolls today. Had our baking contest at the Grange this evening.

Fri 24 – Very cool this morning but warmed up a lot today. I aired more clothes today and washed the closet & wardrobe.

Sat 25 – Fair hot. We were at the Quirin sale, had a flat tire on truck.

Sun 26 – Partly cloudy hot. We stayed home mostly all day this Sunday. Did go to see how the lake was coming along.

Mon 27 – Rained very hard through the night, so I quilted. Anna Frank helped me. We chopped some weeds in evening.

Tues 28 – I worked upstairs and went to Waterloo with Rapps in afternoon to pay our taxes $8.01. I visited with sister Mary awhile.

Wed 29 – Fair hot in the 90s. I hemmed one quilt and worked about the house. Rapps were here in evening.

Thurs 30 – Fair hot 84 at 7 a.m. 98 at 4 p.m. We were at Smithton in morning. Also Irwin was here in evening.

Fri 31 – Fair very hot 102 by late afternoon. I cleaned out the bedroom closet and aired the coats & dresses.

September 1951

Sat 1 – Fair getting cooler, very cool by night. Metzgers took us along to see the parade at Millstadt in evening. Got back home before dark.

Sun 2 – Cloudy and very cool all day 62 degrees. Metzgers took us along to Waterloo to see the parade.

Mon 3 – Cloudy 60 degrees, thundershower by afternoon. We were at Smithton a short while. Bill & Anita were here awhile towards evening.

Tues 4 – Cool all day, 60 in morning, rained all morning. I ironed and worked about the house.

Wed 5 – Rained mostly all day clearing by night. We had the chicken supper committee meeting here in evening.

Thurs 6 – Fair pretty & cool day. Louis & Hattie and Henry & Bertha were here all day. *Louis and Henry Reiss are George's brothers.*

Fri 7 – Fair cool 60 in morning. I worked about the yard & cut lawn. Irv, Mary & children at 10:30 in night.

Sat 8 – Fair to partly cloudy 60 degrees. Mary & Irv went to the South Farm. The children stayed here. Bill, Anita and June Ann had supper with us.

Sun 9 – Cloudy cool 66 in morning. Irwin & Mary and the children left for home by 2 o'clock afternoon. Rained hard by 7 p.m.

Mon 10 – Very cloudy 60 degrees. I worked about the house. We were at Metzgers a short while in afternoon.

Tues 11 – Fair pretty day. I cleaned all the flues in the furnace and the kitchen stove. Then weeded in the yard.

Wed 12 – Fair to cloudy. We got feed ground & mixed at Smithton. Rained hard by evening & most of the night.

Thurs 13 – Fair cool 62 degrees. I washed in the evening. We went to the Grange meeting.

Fri 14 – Fair very pretty day, cool. Alvina Rapp and I were at Belleville to shop for the picnic.

Sat 15 – Partly cloudy & cool all day. I worked about the place, also canned apple sauce.

Sun 16 – Cloudy to fair, cool 54 in morning. The Kruppas were here and brought another quilt for me to quilt.

Mon 17 – Fair, a beautiful day 60 in morning, cool all day. We sat and watched the men build the dam for the lake.

Tues 18 – 59 degrees, fair very pretty day. Mrs. Glauber, Mrs. Reamis, Mrs. Roush, and myself were at the Home Bureau meeting.

Wed 19 – Fair very pretty day, cool in morning. I had the quilts out to air and cut some lawn and dressed 3 chickens.

Thurs 20 – 64 degrees, fair windy form southeast. I dressed 3 chickens for the picnic. We cleaned up the hall. Josephs started to pick corn.

Fri 21 – Fair 65 in morning. Josephs picked corn and took a load 43 bu to Knab's for us. I finished dressing chickens for picnic.

Sat 22 – 52 degrees cloudy, it rained some during the night. We all helped to get the church hall ready for our Grange picnic.

Sun 23 – Cold 42 degrees, fair very pretty day and we had a fine picnic and chicken dinner. Served from one to 7 o'clock p.m. Food was all by then.

Mon 24 – Last night it started to rain as we came home from our picnic at eleven o'clock and it rained hard all night. Today Alvina & I were at Belleville.

Tues 25 – Cloudy all day warmer. We had the checkup meeting here for the chicken dinner, also pasted clipping into scrapbook.

Wed 26 – Fair very windy all day. I canned apple sauce and worked about the place.

Thurs 27 – Cold 42 degrees, fair got up to 65. We cleaned up brush on Schaefer's place. Got the last of the Grimes golden apples. *The "Schaefer place" is 180 acres which includes the Sportsmen's 40 acres that the Reisses bought from the Schaefers in 1917. They still refer to it by the previous owner's name.*

Fri 28 – Fair 43 degrees, stayed cool all day. Josephs finished picking corn.

Sat 29 – Fair 41 degrees, stayed cool all day. I picked up a lot of hickory nuts. Geo & I cleaned up brush on Schaefer's place.

Sun 30 – Fair 52 degrees, very pretty day. Dora Mueth & family were here also Henry & Edna and Vera and Bill, Anita & June Ann. *Edna Lang is Katie's sister and Vera is Henry's and Edna's daughter.*

October 1951

Mon 1 – Fair warm 75 degrees by noon. Josephs combined beans today. Geo & I cut brush & trees along Schaefer's road.

Tues 2 – 65 degrees in morning around 80 by noon. We chopped elm trees & brush on Schaefer's place. Gathered nuts in afternoon.

Wed 3 – Fair hot winds. Geo & I worked along the road cleaning brush. In afternoon I went to Mayestown church doings.

Thurs 4 – Josephs finished hauling beans. Yesterday price was from $2.50 to $2.58, 14% moisture, the field made 174 bu. Total $440.96.

Fri 5 – Fair very warm in morning, cooler by night. I was at Belleville with Joseph to get fertilizer. Guild meeting in evening.

Sat 6 – Very cloudy & light shower. Geo & I finished cleaning brush along wheat ground field. Rained in the afternoon and cooler.

Sun 7 – Very cloudy and cold all day. Bill & June Ann were here for dinner and then they went to the hospital to see Anita.

Mon 8 – Fair 41 degrees. Josephs started sowing fertilizer today 0-2-10. I went to Belleville to see Katie at the hospital. Metzgers took me along.

Tues 9 – 42 degrees, fair to partly cloudy. Josephs started sowing wheat today. We got 2 loads of lime dust from Willard Probst.

Wed 10 – 41 degrees foggy, but fair. Ed & Alvina Feder were here all day. She helped me quilt.

Thurs 11 – 46 degrees, fair. I finished the baby quilt for Mrs. Groth and canned apple sauce. Grange meeting in evening.

Fri 12 – Fair 65 degrees. Franklin, Gerry & boys came in evening also Willie & June Ann. Franklin and Pop & I went to Grange booster meeting.

Sat 13 – Fair very pretty day. We gathered nuts, then after noon we all went to see Aunt Katie at hospital and Anita at Barnes Hospital.

Sun 14 – Fair, gathered more nuts then Willie & June came and we all had Sunday dinner together. After noon they all left for home. Were at Lena Klein's birthday.

Mon 15 – Fair 66 degrees. Roushes took me and Mrs. Dennis to Home Bureau meeting at Mrs. Herman's. Mrs. Dennis gave the minor lesson. Groth baby shower today.

Tues 16 – Fair warm, we picked up apples for cider. Henry Reiss came and spent the afternoon with us.

Wed 17 – Fair warm 70 degrees. Cloudy later in the day. I worked about the house.

Thurs 18 – Fair cool 46 degrees. We cleaned our chicken house and made firewood.

Fri 19 – Cold fair 41 degrees in morning. I canned apple sauce and sewed carpet scraps. Geo & I cleaned brush in afternoon.

Sat 20 – Fair first frost 32 degrees. We got sweet potatoes at Metzgers. I worked about the yard and house.

Sun 21 – Fair hot winds. We were at church. Then we went to Hecker Wurstmarkt with Metzgers. *A wurstmarkt is a large German picnic with beer, bratwurst, and other meats.*

Mon 22 – Rained very hard mostly all day. Rained very hard towards evening. Creeks were out. Franklin drove thru water on coming back.

Tues 23 – Rained mostly all day. I sewed all day. Franklin left for Urbana in the morning.

Wed 24 – Fair cool 54 in morning. I washed. Then we went to Smithton. Irwin, Mary & children came at 9 o'clock evening.

Thurs 25 – Fair, Irwin went to the South farms. In evening after Irv came back, we all went to Bill's house and then to see Anita at the hospital.

Fri 26 – Cloudy to fair. We all visited together till 4:30. Mary & Irv, Steve, Ken & Mary Kay left for Indiana.

Sat 27 – Cloudy raining slowly at times. I worked about the house.

Sun 28 – Fair. Herman & Frank were here. In evening we were at Schilling's.

Mon 29 – We cleaned the chicken house, rained by night. We also brought in firewood.

Tues 30 – Partly cloudy warm. Alma & I were at the quilting at Boeker's. Evening we went to Paderborn card party.

Wed 31 – Very cloudy and rainy all day, turning much colder, 36 in morning. I washed and brought in firewood. Geo made firewood. Snowed by night.

November 1951

Thurs 1 – Cold 32 degrees, fair. We went to Smithton to get car fixed and I got a permanent at Lottie's. In evening we helped peel apples at Koerber's.

Fri 2 – 26 above, snow flurries and strong NW winds, ground frozen hard.

Sat 3 – 16 above in early morning, warmed up to 42 by evening, cloudy, was very stormy all day from south. I patched all day.

Sun 4 – 22 above, cloudy all day. We stayed home all day. Kleins took us along to Gus Metzger's birthday party in evening.

Mon 5 – 27 degrees, very cloudy light coat of snow. Geo & I made firewood all day and I carried it in. Ground was frozen today. I dug up all the cannas & dahlias today. In evening I patched.

Tues 6 – Cold 29 degrees, 12.5 in snow fall during the night, stormy today, roads drifting. Mail carrier left the mail at Klein's. I set up Mrs. Kruppa's quilt today.

Wed 7 – 21 still stormy, snow drifted badly thru the night. Our road is drifted. Mail was at Klein's. I quilted all day.

Thurs 8 – 18 degrees at 8 a.m., warmed up to 37 by noon. Raymond and I walked to Koerber's and went to the Grange meeting with them.

Fri 9 – Partly cloudy, warmer snow melting. I quilted all day.

Sat 10 – 39 degrees, fair, snow is melting. I baked rolls & coffee cake and quilted. Geo made some firewood.

Sun 11 – Fair warm no frost. Bill, Anita & June came and took us along to Hesse's for dinner. This was the first dinner in their new home.

Mon 12 – Rain and strong winds all day. We were at a play at Floraville last night. Today I quilted.

Tues 13 – Fair warm 71 by noon, a thunder shower blew up by 2 p.m., then fair again. I quilted and mixed feed and hauled in wood.

Wed 14 – Josephs butchered today. I helped, was a very nice cool day. Geo made firewood. I hauled it in towards evening.

Thurs 15 – Very cloudy 36 degrees. Geo & I were at Smithton to get feed mixed. Rained towards evening and night. I was to Clara's quilting in evening.

Fri 16 – 25 degrees, snow flurries all day. I quilted all day. Geo couldn't do any outdoors work today.

Sat 17 – 18 above, fair. I quilted and did my Saturday work. Snow flurries in afternoon. We were at Frank Klein's birthday party in evening.

Sun 18 – 18 degrees. Bill, Anita & June were here for dinner. In evening Metzgers took us along to church.

Mon 19 – 20 degrees, fair very pretty day. Roushes & I were to the Home Bureau meeting at Mrs. Carr's in Belleville. In evening I quilted.

Tues 20 – 20 degrees, fair. I finished the Kruppa quilt. Mrs. Carr & Mrs. Roush were here for a short while. Geo made firewood.

Wed 21 – Fair southeast winds 32 in morning. I cleaned the house and Pop made more firewood. Mary & Irwin & children came by 9 o'clock evening.

Thurs 22 – Cloudy all day. Franklin & family came by noon. In evening Bill, Anita and June came and we all had our Thanksgiving turkey dinner together.

Fri 23 – Very cloudy. Gerry, George, Richard & I went to Belleville shopping. Irwin & Franklin went to the south farms. In evening Franklin & family went to Bill's.

Sat 24 – Rained mostly all day. Irwin wasn't feeling good so we stayed indoors. He felt better by evening so we played cards.

Sun 25 – 32 degrees freezing rain thru the night, warmed up to 40 by noon. Bill, Anita & June were here. Irwin & Mary & children left for home.

Mon 26 – 36 degrees, cloudy to fair NW winds. Geo made firewood. I sewed & marked a quilt.

Tues 27 – Fair warm. We were at Millstadt to have the truck tested.

Wed 28 – Fair warmed up to 70 by noon. We cleaned the hen house today. Franklin and Mr. Al Mueller came for supper & stayed overnight.

Thurs 29 – Fair very pretty day. Geo made firewood and crushed corn. I hauled wood in and mixed feed.

Fri 30 – Fair warm 75 by noon. We helped Josephs saw wood and we took some in for the furnace. Franklin and Al Mueller were here for the night.

December 1951

Sat 1 – Franklin & Al Mueller left. Cloudy & warm around 65. Johnny & Jakie patched the chimney. Willie came and took us along home. *John and Jacob Luetzelschwab are Katie's brothers.*

Sun 2 – Partly cloudy & warm all day. We celebrated June Ann's birthday. We came back with Hesse's.

Mon 3 – 62 degrees, light rain, clearing by evening. I marked the second green quilt for Mrs. Hesse.

Tues 4 – Fair very pretty day. I had a quilting party in the evening so I baked cake and pies during the day.

Wed 5 – Cloudy. Franklin came towards evening. Then we all went to the Grange for officers' installation.

Thurs 6 – Cloudy warm windy. I quilted all day. Eliza Koerber helped in the evening. I went to Belleville with Metzgers about taxes.

Fri 7 – Fair very pretty day, warm & windy. I washed a big wash and it all dried.

Sat 8 – Rainy all day. I finished the first green quilt and then put in the second one and quilted quite a bit.

Sun 9 – Cloudy all day, no frost. I quilted. Alma & Gus came in evening to help quilt.

Mon 10 – Cloudy to fair getting colder 32 this morning, very windy all day. I quilted and brought in wood. Geo made firewood.

Tues 11 – Cloudy with snow flurries during afternoon to fair. Mrs. Wachtel and Irene helped me quilt in the evening.

Wed 12 – 30 degrees, ½ inch snow on ground but melted all by night. Mrs. Roush came & helped me quilt. Herbert Neff & Schilling got a Christmas tree.

Thurs 13 – Fair to partly cloudy, 20 degrees in morning, 33 by noon. We were at the Grange meeting, started snowing sleeting & raining after 12 midnight.

Fri 14 – 32 degrees, heavy ice on all trees and ground power line off for 6 hours, trees & limbs breaking down, getting colder since noon.

Sat 15 – 2 above zero, trees, wires still heavy with ice, many trees broken down badly. Didn't get above 9 above all day.

Sun 16 – 5 above, partly cloudy, did not get above 15 all day. Metzgers took us & Raymond along to the Xmas program of the Grange.

Mon 17 – 18 degrees, cloudy to rain & snow by night. Patsy, Mrs. Dennis, Mrs. Roush and I were at Hesse's for Home Bureau.

Tues 18 – 20 degrees, fair. I baked cookies and mixed feed.

Wed 19 – 14 above, fair to cloudy, 21 by noon. Roushes took me along to Belleville for oil meeting. Evening we were at 4H program at Floraville.

Thurs 20 – 35 above, ice melting cloudy and foggy all day. We were at Koerber's birthday party at 11:30. When we went home, it snowed and got much colder.

Fri 21 – 5 above, strong west winds but fair only about an inch of snow. I washed and worked about the house.

Sat 22 – 10 above, fair warmed up to 32. Mary, Irwin & the children got here around 4:30. Then they had supper and went to Bill & Anita's.

Sun 23 – We spent the day at home, fixed up our Christmas tree and got things ready for Christmas.

Mon 24 – Irwin took us all along to the South farms and to his farm. We had a nice trip but cloudy & cold around 27.

Tues 25 – Rainy. Pop, Irwin & I were at church in morning. Afternoon we went to Aunt Katie's then to Bill & Anita's for supper.

Wed 26 – Very cloudy. Anita & June came and got Mary & Mickey. The boys are staying with us. I darned socks.

Thurs 27 – Cloudy cold to 10 above in morning. We went to Grange meeting with Metzgers in evening. Stevie & Kenny went along.

Fri 28 – Cloudy to fair, warmer ice melting some. Geo made firewood, the boys & I hauled it in. Irv and Mary & Mickey came home at night.

Sat 29 – Partly cloudy, warmer, the ice is melting fast. Irwin fixed up both of our cars.

Sun 30 – Very foggy all day, roads thawing out and getting bad. Viola, Ralph & family & Katie were here for dinner. Evening Mary, Irv, Pop & I played cards. *Viola Bald is George's niece. Katie Petry is his sister and the mother of Viola.*

Mon 31 – Very warm, sunshiny all day. Got up to 74. Roads very muddy. We got stuck as we came back from Waterloo.

1952

January 1952

Tues 1 – 36 degrees, NW winds getting colder. Mary & Irwin left for home by 1:30. Bill & Anita were here for dinner then they went to Hesse's.

Wed 2 – 24 degrees, sleet & rain, freezing ice. Clara & Frank Schilling were here in afternoon.

Thurs 3 – 21 degrees cloudy, about ½ in. of sleet & ice on ground. Loretta Probst & Mr. & Mrs. Wm. Schneider were here to help check Ladies Aid books.

Fri 4 – 32 degrees, sleet & rain. I worked on the income tax papers.

Sat 5 – Partly cloudy 32 degrees. We went to Robert Probst's birthday party.

Sun 6 – 30 degrees cloudy all day. Herman & Frank were here for dinner.

Mon 7 – 25 degrees, partly cloudy, rain by night. I brought in some wood. Eliza Koerber, Anna, Frank and I finished the 1951 Grange scrap book.

Tues 8 – 36 degrees, getting warmer. Elmer & Carlena were here yesterday, warmed up to 50. Sunshiney all day. We made firewood.

Wed 9 – 30 degrees, fair. I helped Josephs with the butchering. I bought 17 lbs lard from them.

Thurs 10 – 23 degrees, cloudy. Raymond Joseph got his finger cut off in the tractor. It was cold all day. We went to Grange meeting.

Fri 11 – 29 degrees, warmed up to 42 by afternoon. I mixed feed and worked about the house.

Sat 12 – Fair very pretty day, warm 32 in morning, 50 by noon. We made firewood and brought it in.

Sun 13 – 46 degrees, warmed up to 65 by noon. I was at Belleville Hospital to visit Alma Metzger. She went in yesterday.

Mon 14 – 54 degrees, very cloudy, warm & windy from south all day. I washed a few shirts and cleaned upstairs.

Tues 15 – 54 in morning, 68 by noon, very pretty day. I washed a big wash and it all dried. I washed the upstairs bed things and cleaned the upstairs.

Wed 16 – Partly cloudy 58 degrees, light shower in early morning. I helped clean the hall for the card party. Had a good crowd.

Thurs 17 – 62 degrees in morning, 70 by noon. We helped clean up after the card party.

Fri 18 – Still warm. I cleaned the house. Franklin, Gerry and the boys came at 6 o'clock evening.

Sat 19 – Warm, got up to 71 by noon. Franklin, Gerry, the boys & I were at Belleville in the morning at Red Bud afternoon. Finished income report in evening.

Sun 20 – 32 degrees, strong NW winds but sunshiney all day. Franklin's family left at 1:30 and Bill & Anita came at 3 o'clock. Then Geo & I walked to Roush's for awhile.

Mon 21 – 31 degrees, snowed sleeted and freezing rain mostly all day. I worked about the house.

Tues 22 – 25 degrees getting much colder, very stormy all day. I cut and sewed carpet strips.

Wed 23 – 10 above, fair strong N-west winds. I worked at Roush's, we dressed turkeys.

Thurs 24 – 17 degrees, warmed up to 33 by noon. I was at Schilling's for a little while. We were at Grange meeting in evening.

Fri 25 – 40 degrees cloudy. Geo made firewood. I hauled it in.

Sat 26 – 54 degrees, light rain in early morning to fair & colder by night. I did my Saturday work.

Sun 27 – 35 degrees, cloudy. I was at church. We were at Fred Wachtel's in afternoon.

Mon 28 – 22 degrees, strong NW winds, ½ inch snow by night. I sewed quilt patches. Geo shelled corn by hand.

Tues 29 – 5 above, fair. I cut quilt patches. In evening, Mr. Quirin came and took us to Smithton for the coon supper of the club.

Wed 30 – 11 above, warmed up to 40 by noon. I worked about the house.

Thurs 31 – 30 degrees, warmed up to 54 by noon. I helped with the butchering at Elsie & Albert Hoffman's.

February 1952

Fri 1 – 47 degrees rained a lot during the night. I was at Belleville with Gus Metzger. Irv & Mary & children came at 10 p.m.

Sat 2 – 42 degrees very cloudy, light rains by afternoon. Irwin, Mary and the children left at 12:30 to get to St. Louis and go to California.

Sun 3 – 49 degrees, rained all night and all day today. So we spent the Sunday at home.

Mon 4 – Rained slowly all day. I started to set a quilt together.

Tues 5 – 32 degrees white frost, very pretty day but rain by night. Raymond & we were at card party. Alma & I marked & set up our quilt.

Wed 6 – 28 degrees, cloudy after an early morning drizzle. Alma & I quilted some more on our Grange quilt.

Thurs 7 – 22 degrees, fair. I quilted at Alma's. Got the news that Aunt Katie had passed away last night at 7:20 Feb 6th. *John Luetzelschwab is Katie's brother and "Aunt" Katie was his wife.*

Fri 8 – Frost in the morning, warmed up nicely during the day. Raymond took us to Millstadt. We went to the funeral home to see Aunt Katie. Franklin came in evening.

Sat 9 – Light frost, very pretty day, windy. We all were at Aunt Katie's funeral. Had supper with Bill & Anita. Roads were dried off nicely.

Sun 10 – Light frost, fair very pretty day. We all went to church at Millstadt. Franklin & family left for home after dinner. We were at Boobie Klein's in evening.

Mon 11 – Fair very pretty day. I raked part of the lawn and mixed feed. Geo crushed corn and made firewood.

Tues 12 – Cloudy white frost 31 degrees, little shower by afternoon. I helped Alma quilt, then took quilt home. We & Raymond went to card party with Metzgers.

Wed 13 – 46 degrees, thundershower to fair by afternoon. I worked about the house.

Thurs 14 – 35 degrees, cloudy. I quilted. We & Raymond were at Grange meeting in evening.

Fri 15 – Very cloudy 32 degrees. Joseph & I were at Smithton to sign up for farm program. Alma & I finished the quilt in afternoon.

Sat 16 – 30 degrees very cloudy all day & damp cold. I did my Saturday work & brought wood in. Geo crushed corn.

Sun 17 – 30 degrees, fair very pretty day. We spent the Sunday here at home.

Mon 18 – Fair 32 degrees. Geo made firewood. I darned socks and hauled in wood.

Tues 19 – Fair to cloudy, thundershower by night. I helped Mrs. Walter Brandenburger with quilting. In evening we were at Woodman card party.

Wed 20 – 34 degrees clear strong NW winds all day. I washed and ironed.

Thurs 21 – 24 degrees, cold NW winds, fair. Henry Kampe's house burned today. I baked cookies, Geo & Raymond went to Kampe's.

Fri 22 – 32 degrees, snowed all day but melted as it fell. Mrs. Joseph & Raymond, Geo & I went to Smithton card party.

Sat 23 – 34 degrees, very cloudy, cloudy all day. Mary & Irwin and the children came back from Calif. At around 3 o'clock afternoon.

Sun 24 – Cloudy. We all went to Millstadt to see Johnny & Rollie's family for a short while. Then at eleven o'clock Mary & Irv & children left for home. *John Luetzelschwab is Katie's brother and Rollie is John's son.*

Mon 25 – Fair 27 degrees. I had a bad cold so I didn't do much work. Brother Johnny is staying with us at nights this week.

Tues 26 – 22 degrees. I went quilting at Fred Wachtel's.

Wed 27 – Fair 32 degrees. Alma & I went quilting at Barthel's. Irwin came in the evening and stayed overnight.

Thurs 28 – Fair 50 degrees. Irwin left for Canton this morning. Johnny went to work at Millstadt. Fire close to the Schaefer land.

Fri 29 – Very cloudy light rain at times. I was at church in evening with Metzgers. Boobie & Schillings worked hard to put out the fire last night along the Schaefer land.

March 1952

Sat 1 – Very cloudy all day, raw east wind. Bill, Anita & June Ann were here for supper. I set up a quilt today. 32 degrees in morning.

Sun 2 – 33 degrees, snowing about 2 in on the ground melted by noon. Sister Edna & Myrtle were here in afternoon.

Mon 3 – Raining getting colder very foggy as Johnny came back from work. I patched & mixed feed. Geo made firewood.

Tues 4 – 24 in morning, strong NW winds & snow flurries. I sewed quilt patches all day.

Wed 5 – 13 above, fair. I worked on the quilt all day.

Thurs 6 – 18 above, fair. I sewed on my quilt. Geo made firewood.

Fri 7 – 33 above, fair. I worked about the house.

Sat 8 – 39 degrees. We cleaned the chicken house today. Then went to the 4H card party.

Sun 9 – 44 warmed up to 69 by afternoon. We went to church then stayed home all day. Rain by night.

Mon 10 – 48 degrees, rained all day. I quilted mostly all day.

Tues 11 – 45 in morning, fair very pretty day. I washed and ironed and quilted awhile. Geo made firewood.

Wed 12 – 33 degrees, white frost, fair to cloudy. Clara S. was here also Mr. & Mrs. Roush. Raymond and we were to Pomona meeting. Rained hard.

Thurs 13 – 38 degrees, very windy from NW ending by night. We and Raymond were to Grange meeting.

Fri 14 – 35 degrees, very cloudy, snow by night. We made firewood and hauled it in in evening. Albert & Elsie were here.

Sat 15 – 28 degrees, 2 inch snow, clearing. Did my Saturday work.

Sun 16 – 29 degrees, white frost. We stayed home all day. In evening we were at the family night supper at Floraville.

Mon 17 – 28 degrees, ground frozen. I washed. Then we went to the Home Bureau meeting at Herr's. Mary & Lillian were here & stayed overnight.

Tues 18 – Rained mostly all day, cold 38. Mary & Lillian stayed over night again. We quilted.

Wed 19 – 46 in morning, fair warmed up to 60 by noon. I was at Belleville with Metzgers. I bought oil cloth for the kitchen floor, also a chair for myself.

Thurs 20 – Fair to cloudy, warm and nice to work outdoors. We made firewood. In evening Koerbers took us along to Minstrel.

Fri 21 – Cloudy all day, rain towards evening. We planted 125 pine trees on hill by Roush's.

Sat 22 – 48 degrees, raining, getting stormy & colder by afternoon. Bill & Anita and June Ann came towards evening. Franklin & Rich also came.

Sun 23 – 25 degrees, fair. Henry & Bertha, Bill & Rose, Bill, Anita and June Ann came for dinner. We celebrated my birthday. Bill & Franklin planted pine trees.

Mon 24 – 28 degrees fair, got nice & warm during the day. Franklin went in the evening to a meeting at Sparta. Richard & I baked a cake & packed eggs.

Tues 25 – 36 degrees, a pretty day, got windy & colder by afternoon. Franklin & Richard left for home. Pearl & Melvin & children came in evening. *Pearl Schuchardt is Katie's niece. She was the daughter of Katie's sister Lena Speichinger but was adopted and raised by Katie's brother John Luetzelschwab shortly after Pearl's father died in 1927.*

Wed 26 – 30 degrees, jack frost. Planted trees & washed and were to the Sportsmen's meeting in evening.

Thurs 27 – 32 degrees white frost. I raked & burned brush by the chicken yard and planted pine trees. Were at Grange meeting in evening.

Fri 28 – 33 degrees, planted more pine trees and pruned peach trees and cleaned up around the chicken yard.

Sat 29 – 48 degrees, warmed up to 75. Mrs. Barthel & I were at the home of Mrs. Tieberend for a Pomona Home Ec meeting.

Sun 30 – 48 degrees, windy all day. We were at church. Afternoon I prepared for my birthday party. 26 people were here.

Mon 31 – 56 degrees, windy partly cloudy. We worked about the place. Thunder and rain & some hail by night.

April 1952

Tues 1 – 50 degrees, cloudy. I planted 25 pine trees along the north fence of chicken yard. Afternoon I was to a quilting at Kempp's.

Wed 2 – Fair 42 degrees, NW winds. Bill & Anita were here last night. They got their meat at Knab's. I washed today. Geo planted trees.

Thurs 3 – I set up the quilt for Knab's. I also helped Geo make firewood. Rained by night and all night.

Fri 4 – 42, rained all day. I quilted all day.

Sat 5 – 36 degrees, NW winds cloudy all day and cold. I quilted mostly all day.

Sun 6 – 36 degrees, cloudy to fair, NWest winds. We were at church, then I quilted. Bill & Anita came in afternoon.

Mon 7 – Fair getting warmer. I raked and burned brush. Geo planted pine trees & made firewood.

Tues 8 – 70 degrees by noon. I raked more around the outside yard. Johnny came to stay overnight. We were at Smithton.

Wed 9 – 46 in morning, partly cloudy, warmed up to 81 for a short time. In evening it rained and turned much cooler 35 by 10 p.m.

Thurs 10 – 34 degrees, fair stayed cool all day. We were at Grange meeting.

Fri 11 – 36 degrees, very cloudy all day, rain by night. We prepared for our trip to Mary and Irwin's.

Sat 12 – 44 degrees, raining. We are about ready to leave for East St. Louis at 7:30, arrived at Vincennes, Ind. at 4 p.m.

Sun 13 – Still raining. Mary & Irwin got us at the bus station yesterday afternoon, rained all night. Irwin and I were at church, all rested after noon.

Mon 14 – Still more rain colder, light snow in early morning, melted as quick as it fell. Mary ironed, I patched. Irv was at the office.

Tues 15 – Clearing 40 degrees. We patched again. We enjoyed our visit with our children.

Wed 16 – Fair very pretty day, we all worked about the yard while Mary, Irv & Kenny went to see the doctor for Ken's ear.

Thurs 17 – Fair warm, very pretty day. We cleaned around the place and planted flowers.

Fri 18 – Fair warm. We took the train home, got to E. St. Louis at 12:25. Bill & Anita got us and we stayed overnight.

Sat 19 – Fair warm. Bill, Anita and June took us home and had supper with us.

Sun 20 – Fair warm. Geo & I were at Vera's wedding today. I helped with the cooking. Johnny took us home and stayed overnight.

Mon 21 – 60 degrees, raining, quit by noon. Mrs. Glauber, Mrs. Dennis and I were at the Home Bureau meeting today.

Tues 22 – Partly cloudy to fair, rain at night. Uncle Henry was here all day. Johnny came in the evening.

Wed 23 – Fair getting cooler 48 by night. I washed & ironed some. Spent the afternoon with Clara Schilling.

Thurs 24 – Cloudy & cold 43 in morning. I and Mrs. Joseph hewed the sill for the barn. Then I baked coffee cake. We were at the Grange meeting in evening.

Fri 25 – Fair 47 degrees, windy. I cut the lawn and quilted some also transplanted some of the house plants.

Sat 26 – Fair hot. I cleaned the house and baked 2 cakes. Were at Joseph's 30th wedding anniversary in the evening.

Sun 27 – Fair very pretty day. We were at Bill & Rose's for dinner with Bill, Anita & June. Birthday club came in evening.

Mon 28 – Fair hot. I worked in the garden and cleaned up after Geo's birthday party.

Tues 29 – Fair hot. I washed & ironed. Spaded garden, planted the first beans and lettuce. I was at the quilt piecing for the contest.

Wed 30 – 62 degrees, 84 by noon. I planted flower seeds & glads. We were at the Tom Brenneman show at Smithton in evening.

May 1952

Thurs 1 – 60 degrees in morning, 85 by noon. We got the concrete mix for the hog floor. John & Jakie also put a new sill in the barn.

Fri 2 – Fair hot. I spaded and planted more beans & flower seeds. Geo planted pine trees.

Sat 3 – Fair hot 88 degrees by noon. I mowed the lawn and baked cake & rolls.

Sun 4 – Fair hot 92 by 4:30 p.m. We were at church then in evening we were at Boobie Klein's.

Mon 5 – Fair hot 92 by noon. I worked in the garden. We took the eggs to Smithton in the morning & visited Mrs. Halfrick.

Tues 6 – Fair cooler, had a nice shower last night. The Floraville Home Bureau was organized today with 14 members.

Wed 7 – Cloudy to fair, not so hot. I spaded a lot and planted dahlias & cannas.

Thurs 8 – Very cool, cloudy, hard rain by night, thundering a lot. We were at Belleville with business. Were at Grange meeting in evening.

Fri 9 – 59 degrees fair. I worked in garden. We also bought 10 spring chickens of Wachtel's, butchered them to put in deep freeze.

Sat 10 – Rainy part of the day, very cool 55 degrees, fair & cooler by night.

Sun 11 – Cloudy stormy from NW, showers now & then. We were at church.

Mon 12 – Fair, cold 46 in morning. We took more dressed chickens to the deep freeze. Bill, Anita & Rosemarie were here in evening.

Tues 13 – Fair very cool, 52 degrees. Metzgers took us along to Belleville for Geo's eye test.

Wed 14 – 56 degrees, partly cloudy to fair. Ida Gasser, Emma Barthel and I were to the annual Home Bureau meeting at Pres. Church. Pomona meeting in evening.

Thurs 15 – 64 degrees, fair getting much warmer. I planted cucumbers today and flowers and seed.

Fri 16 – 64 in morning. I cut lawn. Roushes were here a while, also Henry & Harold Lang. I canned 6 pints pineapples.

Sat 17 – 58 degrees, cloudy all day. I picked 5 quarts strawberries and cut lawn and baked rolls & coffee cake.

Sun 18 – I was in church. Metzgers took us along to Shiloh Valley Grange strawberry social and cold supper. Light rains during day.

Mon 19 – Cloudy very cool. We started to chop trees & brush along branch in Schaefer's bottom.

Tues 20 – Still cool 50 degrees. We chopped more trees & brush in morning. Afternoon I picked strawberries, 1 ½ gal in orchard.

Wed 21 – Cool 54 degrees in morning. Langs cut clover for hay. We cut more brush.

Thurs 22 – Getting warmer. We worked along the branch again. Were to Grange meeting in evening.

Fri 23 – Light drizzle through the day, warmer. I washed and cut weeds.

Sat 24 – Fair. We worked in bottom, burned brush piles. A bad thunderstorm came up in evening and rained very hard.

Sun 25 – Cloudy all day. Bill, Anita & June were for dinner. Lottie & Ed came afternoon. Marcella & Boobie came in evening. *Lottie Sander is Katie's sister.*

Mon 26 – Fair, hot 85 by noon. We burned brush in bottom. Were at Floraville in evening for school graduation.

Tues 27 – Fair. We cleaned up along the mailbox bottom. Langs bailed hay. I hoed in my garden in afternoon & picked strawberries.

Wed 28 – Raining lightly, 60 degrees. Alma and I helped clean the preacher's house. Went to the graduation at Smithton in evening.

Thurs 29 – Fair. I cut the lawn and worked about the place. Irwin, Mary & children came in afternoon. Marie Standley's party in evening.

Fri 30 – Fair. Mary & Irwin & Steven left for their trip south this morning. Rollie & Barbara & children & Johnny came in afternoon. *John Luetzelschwab is Katie's brother and Rollie is John's son.*

Sat 31 – We did our Saturday work. Bill & Anita came in evening. Irwin called in evening.

June 1952

Sun 1 – Very pretty day. We were at our strawberry social. Willie Feders took us home & stayed awhile. *William Feder is George's first cousin who lives in Belleville, Illinois.*

Mon 2 – Fair cool. Mary Kay had fever so I didn't do much besides taking care of her.

Tues 3 – Fair hot 89 degrees. I cut weeds. Henry & Edna came in evening. Floyd Mueller got some hay. Clara Schilling was here.

Wed 4 – Fair. I cut a lot of weeds. Then Johnny came and put up our awnings on the windows. He brought cherries. I canned 4.5 quarts.

Thurs 5 – Hot 95 degrees by 3 p.m. Uncle Henry & Roushes were here for dinner. I washed in the morning. Irwin called in evening. *Henry Reiss is George's brother in St. Louis.*

Fri 6 – Fair very hot all day, 92 by afternoon. I darned socks and took care of the children.

Sat 7 – Very hot 98 degrees. Irwin & Mary & Stevie came back from Florida. In evening we went to Alma Metzger's birthday party.

Sun 8 – Fair hot 95 by noon. Bill & Anita & June came and had dinner with us. Irwin & Mary left for home afternoon. Franklin & Gerry & boys came.

Mon 9 – Rained very hard during the night but fair & hot today. We all went to Belleville to shop.

Tues 10 – Fair hot around 96. Franklin & Gerry helped lay the kitchen oil cloth. Bill & Anita were here for supper. They went boat riding (*probably at the new Sportsmen's Lake*).

Wed 11 – Fair hot 99 by afternoon. Franklin & Gerry were at Bill & Anita's overnight. Came home this evening. Johnny was here for supper.

Thurs 12 – Fair hot 100 by afternoon. We were at Forest Park. Had supper at Bill & Anita's. In evening we got things ready to go to Urbana in morning.

Fri 13 – Fair hot 99. We left at 6:30 a.m. arrived at Urbana at around eleven o'clock. Rained hard there that night.

Sat 14 – Partly cloudy hot 99 degrees. Bill & Anita came by afternoon. I picked the strawberries. Gerry prepared for the next day.

Sun 15 – Fair hot. Today was 102 degrees, hottest day of our lives. Franklin's graduation. Went to Sunday school & church and took picture. Mary & Irwin came. *Franklin Reiss received his doctorate degree from the University of Illinois, College of Agriculture. He spent his career there teaching agricultural economics.*

Mon 16 – Fair hot 102 by afternoon. I was at the Home Bureau meeting at Mrs. Dennis'.

Tues 17 – Fair not so hot. Cooled off during the night. I started to clean the sun porch. Geo cleaned brush along the road.

Wed 18 – Fair 68 in early morning, still washing & cleaning the sun porch. Geo is chopping off trees along corn land.

Thurs 19 – 95 by afternoon. I finished washing the porch walls. Planted a few sweet potatoes.

Fri 20 – Fair to cloudy good shower by 2:30 p.m. Mary & Irv came by 6 in the evening. Johnny also came and stayed overnight.

Sat 21 – Fair, hot. Mary, Irwin & Ken left for Nebraska this morning. Mary Kay & Stevie stay with us.

Sun 22 – Partly cloudy all day, light shower towards evening. Mr. & Mrs. Dennis & family were here in evening. Elmer Kaburecks were here afternoon. *George and Katie also owned a separate 40 acres about five miles southwest. Elmer Kabureck was their farm tenant on that parcel.*

Mon 23 – Fair. Got up to 99 by 4 p.m. I washed and patched. The children played indoors most of the day. Joseph tried to combine wheat today.

Tues 24 – Hot winds all day. I ironed and patched. Joseph combined the Kuhn's corner. Made about 17 bu to acre.

Wed 25 – 80 degrees at 7:30 a.m. 101 degrees at 3 p.m. Hot winds all day. Josephs are combining.

Thurs 26 – Hot 104 by 4 p.m. Couldn't do much outdoors.

Fri 27 – Hot 103 by late afternoon, had a good shower. Mary & Irwin & Kenny came back from Nebraska trip.

Sat 28 – Still hot 101 by afternoon. Mary painted our bathroom and porch.

Sun 29 – Very hot today 104 to 105. We all left for Sullivan at 10 a.m. Got there by 3 p.m.

Mon 30 – Fair hot. Mary went to the hospital at Terre Haute in the afternoon. I kept the children and ironed.

July 1952

Tues 1 – Fair hot around 99. Irwin was with Mary mostly all day as she was getting her treatments.

Wed 2 – Still hot. Irwin took the children & me to see Mary at the hospital.

Thurs 3 – Cooler thundering and raining slowly all day. Turned very cool that night.

Fri 4 – 66 degrees, fair. We weeded some flowers and I washed. We saw the fireworks at the park. Also baked coffee cake

Sat 5 – Fair still cool. I cleaned the house and did more weeding.

Sun 6 – Fair getting much hotter. Mary came home from the hospital at noon. The children were at Sunday School.

Mon 7 – Very hot 101 at noon. We came back by train to E. St. Louis at 1:20. Bill & Anita got us and we had supper at their house.

Tues 8 – Light rain and much cooler thru the night, 64 in morning. I washed and we went to Floraville Home Bureau meeting in afternoon.

Wed 9 – Fair 66 degrees in morning around 85 by noon. I ironed and patched. Went to see Clara Schilling in afternoon. Johnny & Ed & Rose Keim were here in evening.

Thurs 10 – 67 in early morning, 88 by afternoon. I cleaned upstairs. Were to Grange meeting in evening.

Fri 11 – Cool in morning 68, 99 by 4 p.m., hot winds. I washed and patched. We got a new battery for coupe today.

Sat 12 – Very hot around 100 by afternoon. We got meat at Knab's. Then I baked rolls & coffee cake.

Sun 13 – Partly cloudy, very stormy, hot around 98 by noon. We were at church. Boobie Kleins & Elmer Kaburecks were here. Rain by night.

Mon 14 – Raining slowly. Rained during the night. Alma & Gus were here yesterday evening.

Tues 15 – Shower. I chopped weeds and worked in the house.

Wed 16 – Fair hot by noon, light rain in the night. I was at Millstadt with Josephs.

Thurs 17 – Fair not so hot. Johnny was with us overnight. I went to Walter Kindaur's funeral with Metzgers.

Fri 18 – Fair hot winds all day, 95 by afternoon, 90 at 6 p.m. I cleaned the living room.

Sat 19 – Fair hot. I baked cake and rolls and cleaned the house.

Sun 20 – Fair hot winds. We were in church. Baked cake for my meeting tomorrow. Brandenbergers were here in evening.

Mon 21 – Fair hot 95 by 3 p.m. The Prairie & Floraville units met here also present were 20 children and 2 visitors, 60 in all.

Tues 22 – Fair hot 98 by afternoon. Alma & I quilted on contest quilt at Kruppa's. Boobie took us along to school meeting in Smithton in evening.

Wed 23 – Fair hot to much cooler by night. We quilted on the chance quilt today. I took it home in evening. We paid 89 cents tax on the Arkansas plot. Got the receipt today.

Thurs 24 – Fair cool 69 degrees in morning, 93 by afternoon. Uncle Henry spent the day with us. Grange meeting in evening. Received AAA check $61.20.

Fri 25 – Hot. Harold got us and we went to Mrs. Gummersheimer's funeral. Also dressed 3 chickens. *Mrs. Gummersheimer was the mother-in-law of Katie's sister Caroline.*

Sat 26 – Hot. We swept & cleaned up a little at the new Grange hall in morning. Mrs. Roush helped quilt afternoon. 100 at noon, 105 by 4 p.m., 102 at 6 p.m. We went to see parade at Smithton.

Sun 27 – Hot 75 in morning, 105 by noon. Johnny and Westerheides were here. 108 afternoon. We went to Smithton Homecoming with Alma & Gus in evening.

Mon 28 – 80 in early morning. Hot winds. We took dressed chickens to Roush deep freeze, then stayed indoors & quilted. 106 all afternoon.

Tues 29 – 85 degrees at 8 o'clock a.m. Thundered all last night but very little rain.

Wed 30 – Fair around 90 to 93. We went to the Belleville Fair with Metzgers. Washed in evening.

Thurs 31 – Fair hot around 90. Irwin, Mary and the children came at about 3 o'clock. Irwin went to Denmark Farms in evening.

August 1952

Fri 1 – Fair hot, some rain by night. Langs cut last clover seed. Irwin came back in evening. We didn't do much work, just visited.

Sat 2 – Fair cooler. Bill, Anita & June were here for supper.

Sun 3 – Not so hot, but a good shower by night. I helped at the Neff Golden Wedding celebration. Mary took Irwin to station at St. Louis.

Mon 4 – Fair cool. Mary & the children stayed at Bill & Anita's last night. Came home at 10 a.m. today. Took me to Freeburg. Had all my upper teeth pulled.

Tues 5 – Cool. We went to Marcella's for a short while. Then we laid rocks by our yard gate.

Wed 6 – Rained slowly all night. Plowing goes good now. Josephs started to plow today. Mary, the children & I went to St. Louis to get Irwin as he came back from Texas.

Thurs 7 – Fair cool, 65 in morning. Irwin, Mary & children left for home then I washed and then went to Kemp's to help quilt.

Fri 8 – Partly cloudy all day 95 by noon, 75 in morning. I baked cake and cleaned some. Also peeled some peaches. Mr. Ehret & Mr. Leiner paid $20 for hunting on Schaefer place.

Sat 9 – Fair cool. Franklin, Gerry, George & Richard came at 5:30 to spend the week with us.

Sun 10 – Fair, cool all day. We spent the day with Henry & Bertha. Had supper at Bill & Anita's.

Mon 11 – Rained slowly all morning. We all went to Freeburg as I had to go to Dr. Gorden. Then we went to Edwin & Beulah's.

Tues 12 – We were at Waterloo for dinner at Aunt Mary's. Also stopped at Carlena's and Pearl's for a short while.

Wed 13 – We went to Dr. Gorden then to Belleville. Were at the Progressive Grange in evening. Pearl & Melvin visited here with the children.

Thurs 14 – We didn't do much work. Went to Grange meeting in evening. Franklin & Richard cleaned around the pond. Gerry & George were at show.

Fri 15 – Fair, not so hot. We were on the boat today. Rained a shower by night. Our electric was off from 6 p.m. till 10 a.m. Sat.

Sat 16 – Fair rather warm. I baked rolls & coffee cake. Franklin & Geo & Richard went horseback riding at Roush's.

Sun 17 – Fair. Franklin, Gerry & boys left to go to Bill & Anita's and left for home the next day. We were at church, then Freeburg Homecoming in evening.

Mon 18 – Cloudy all day. I canned peaches all day. Langs plowed.

Tues 19 – Fair, hot around 90. I washed. Then the boys brought me peaches. So I canned peaches till late in evening.

Wed 20 – Fair, hot 85 by noon. I ironed and helped Mrs. Roush peel peaches. Patched in evening.

Thurs 21 – Raining lightly. I cleaned up about the house, dressed Robert Schneider's chickens for the picnic.

Fri 22 – 65 degrees, did not get above 80 all day. I canned 15 quarts of peaches, those that Herman brought.

Sat 23 – Cool 61 degrees in morning, very pretty day for our Grange picnic. Sold around 325 meal tickets.

Sun 24 – We were at church first, then we cleaned up at the hall. 60 degrees in morning. Herman brought me about 2 bu peaches. Johnny was here with his new car.

Mon 25 – 64 degrees, 90 by noon. We were at Schilling's a short while. Rudy went to the hospital and was operated at 8 o'clock evening.

Tues 26 – 68 in morning, 93 by noon. I canned peaches then helped Marcella peel peaches.

Wed 27 – Hot in the 90s during the day. I canned peaches, have 70 quarts now. I went to the chicken supper committee meeting in evening. We cleared $895.

Thurs 28 – Fair hot. Canned damsons. Painters made a start on the granary shed. I helped Mrs. Roush peel peaches. Johnny was here in evening.

Fri 29 – Fair 90 by noon. The painters are painting the house & barn over on the Joseph's place, also shed roofs with zinc.

Sat 30 – Cloudy light drizzle for about a half hour. The men finished the paint job this morning. We & Metzgers went to Millstadt Homecoming in evening.

Sun 31 – 70 degrees, 90 by noon. We were at Metzger's also Dara Mueth's & family. Bill, Anita & June also came toward evening.

September 1952

Mon 1 – Very cloudy to fair & hot, thundery by 3 p.m. Rained hard by night. I chopped weeds & we made some firewood. Edgar, Ellen & Earl were here awhile. *Edgar Luetzelschwab is Katie's nephew. Ellen* *and Earl are his children.*

Tues 2 – Fair cold 54 in morning. Pop & I cut trees & brush by the 8 acres. Afternoon I washed. Mrs. Roush was here awhile.

Wed 3 – 50 degrees stayed cool all day. We chopped brush & trees in morning. I ironed in afternoon and patched.

Thurs 4 – 50 degrees in morning but warmed up by afternoon. We cut more trees, then Raymond & I went to Smithton.

Fri 5 – Fair 54 in morning, 93 by noon. Pop & I chopped trees & brush.

Sat 6 – 54 in morning, 93 by noon. Henry Lang helped us saw off some of the large trees by the 8 acres. Harold disked the land. *The 8 acres is the old sheep pasture just east of the barn.*

Sun 7 – 62 degrees cloudy to clearing. We stayed home all day. I baked pies & a cake.

Mon 8 – 55 degrees in morning, warmed up to 88. We were to the funeral of Mrs. Emma Klein at Floraville. We chopped trees in the morning. Oil lease check $159. *George had bought 160 acres of cotton land sight unseen in the Texas panhandle in 1907. That parcel was leased several years for oil exploration but there is not evidence a well was ever drilled or even discovered in the area.*

Tues 9 – Fair hot 92 by noon. We chopped brush & trees along the 8 acres. Afternoon I quilted.

Wed 10 – Fair hot 93 by noon. We chopped trees & brush. Went to Pomona meeting at night with Orville & Marie to Emerald Mound Grange.

Thurs 11 – Hot 95 by noon. Mrs. Dennis & I went to Belleville with Ida Gasser to take Home Bureau lesson. Were at Grange meeting in evening.

Fri 12 – Fair hot 95 by noon. We chopped brush & trees in morning. Afternoon I canned some cling peaches. Johnny brought some tomatoes.

Sat 13 – Fair windy 92 by noon. Partly cloudy. We chopped brush awhile then I did my Saturday work. Canned some cling peaches.

Sun 14 – Partly cloudy 71 in morning. We were at church. Johnny came in evening. Had a good shower.

Mon 15 – Fair cool. We chopped trees. Franklin came in evening.

Tues 16 – Fair. Franklin & I were at Belleville in morning. Franklin made his Booster Night talk at the Grange. We got a large load of Raw Rock on field in front of our house, also some back of orchard.

Wed 17 – Partly cloudy. Franklin left for home. Rained hard at 3 a.m. Irwin was here for dinner. Then he went home. Clara came afternoon.

Thurs 18 – Fair, warmed up to 80 by noon. We worked about the yard. Afternoon I went to Home Bureau meeting at Progressive Grange.

Fri 19 – Fair, 52 degrees, NW wind. We chopped trees in morning then I canned grapes & jelly. Got 2 loads of Raw Rock, one load on Henry's field on Schaefer's place & one load on the 20 acres land or 0.5 ton to each field.

Sat 20 – 53 degrees fair, cloudy by afternoon, light rain by 3 p.m. I cooked jelly and chili sauce.

Sun 21 – 59 degrees. We went to church. Bill & Anita & June Ann were here for dinner. Afternoon we went to Camp Vanderwert at Waterloo.

Mon 22 – 46 degrees fair. Anita took me to the dentist and we had dinner at Mrs. Hesse's. Mrs. Joseph went to the hospital. She is bad sick.

Tues 23 – 42 degrees, fair.

Wed 24 – 47 degrees, fair. I went to the Red Bud Hospital to see Mrs. Joseph. Then I painted yard fence. H. Lang hauled over firewood.

Thurs 25 – 47 degrees, fair. Were at Grange meeting in evening.

Fri 26 – 53 degrees, fair. I painted yard fence. Afternoon I helped to varnish at the Grange. Were at Broad Hollow Grange Booster Night in evening.

Sat 27 – 47 degrees. I painted on yard fence in morning. Afternoon I helped varnish at the Grange. Were to a moving picture at church in evening.

Sun 28 – 60 in morning. We were at the Sportsmen's wurstmarkt with Bill & Anita. At church affair in evening.

Mon 29 – 65 in morning, 90 by noon. I washed and patched.

Tues 30 – 60 in early morning, hot during the day. Bill & Anita came and took me to the dentist. Got my teeth today.

October 1952

Wed 1 – Hot got up to 94 by noon. I chopped weeds and we both made some firewood.

Thurs 2 – Windy from the north, 52 in morning. I spent the day with Mrs. Joseph at Red Bud Hospital. Franklin came in evening.

Fri 3 – 33 degrees. Tomatoes & sweet potatoes frozen. Henry Lang started sowing wheat yesterday and finished today. All hard wheat.

Sat 4 – Partly cloudy, cool all day. I started to clean the feed house and baked pies.

Sun 5 – 52 degrees, very cloudy, raining slowly by afternoon. We were at church. Johnny took the awnings off this morning. Metzgers & we were at Margret Probst's birthday.

Mon 6 – 33 degrees, fair NW winds. I cleaned the feed house and clipped flowers & took them in as it was getting colder.

Tues 7 – 29 degrees, heavy white frost, all plants frozen. I washed today. Mrs. Dennis & Mrs. Glauber were here in afternoon.

Wed 8 – Fair 33 degrees. I potted house plants. In evening we were at Pomona meeting at Bob White Grange.

Thurs 9 – 35 degrees, fair, warmed up nicely during the day. I went to the church meeting with Mrs. Barthel to Waterloo. Grange meeting in evening.

Fri 10 – 36 degrees. Potted more plants in morning. Afternoon we went to help clean up basement at the new Grange.

Sat 11 – 36 degrees, fair. I baked and did my Saturday work. Johnny brought us poulets from Tilli. In evening he called & said Betty Rahe's husband died.

Sun 12 – Fair 50 degrees, we were at church. Bill & Anita came toward evening. Then later they took us to Lena Klein's birthday party.

Mon 13 – 69 degrees in morning, 88 by noon, windy & very dusty. Josephs sowed the wheat in front of the house. Geo & I cleaned out the corn crib.

Tues 14 – Fair cooler 54 in morning, cloudy by noon, getting colder. We had a shower for Mrs. Glauber today at the Floraville Home Bureau meeting.

Wed 15 – Cold, had a good shower during the night. We shelled more corn and I hauled wood in.

Thurs 16 – Fair very pretty day. I mixed feed & worked about the place. Brought in some of the potted plants. 35 degrees in morning.

Fri 17 – Fair turning colder, 37 in morning. I brought all the flowers in and dug the cannas. Metzgers took us along to Broad Hollow Grange program.

Sat 18 – Fair cold 32 degrees. I raked part of the outside yard then I washed Johnny's wash.

Sun 19 – Fair 50 degrees, stayed cool all day. We were at church then Herman & Frank were here for dinner. Metzgers & we went to see Mrs. Wirth at the hospital at Red Bud.

Mon 20 – 37 degrees getting colder. Ida Gasser took me & Mrs. Dennis to Ellen Werner's Home Bureau meeting. We gave the lesson.

Tues 21 – Fair 21 degrees, hard freeze, leaves are falling fast. I raked leaves all morning. Were at Woodmen card party in evening.

Wed 22 – 23 degrees fair. We burned brush in chicken yard. Afternoon I worked in the house. Albert, Elsie & Harvey were here in evening.

Thurs 23 – Fair warmer. I cleaned everything. Mary & Irwin and the children came at 3:30.

Fri 24 – We all went to Irwin's farm today, had our lunch along. It was hot all day around 80.

Sat 25 – Fair 85 by noon. We were at the lake awhile. In evening we had a supper for Mary Kay's birthday.

Sun 26 – Fair hot 80 by noon. Mary & Irv left for home after noon. Bill & Anita then took us to our Dedication of our Grange.

Mon 27 – Getting much colder. I set up a quilt, also visited Clara awhile. Lawrence Klein was operated on today. In evening we cleaned up at Grange.

Tues 28 – 22 degrees. I quilted all day. Strong NW winds.

Wed 29 – Fair. I quilted all day. I had a head cold. Geo stayed in the house. Still cold 30 this morning.

Thurs 30 – Fair 36 degrees. I have a cold and Mrs. Joseph was very sick with stomach flu so I stayed with her awhile. Henry came for dinner.

Fri 31 – 43 degrees, fair. I washed. Geo made firewood. Then I quilted.

November 1952

Sat 1 – 45 degrees, fair. I quilted a lot. Jakie & Cora got 9 bu wheat towards evening. *Jacob Luetzelschwab is Katie's brother.*

Sun 2 – 55 degrees, partly cloudy to cooler by night. Johnny got us and we went to Elmer & Carlena's for the day. Evening Gus Metzger's birthday. *Caroline (Carlena in German) Gummersheimer is Katie's sister.*

Mon 3 – 47 degrees, fair. I was at Columbia with Josephs. I bought a suit for Geo. Afternoon I quilted.

Tues 4 – Fair 30 degrees. We went voting with Metzgers. After that I quilted and finished it in the evening.

Wed 5 – 48 degrees. I washed windows and then put in the storm windows. Then I cleaned upstairs.

Thurs 6 – 33 degrees, windy all day. I washed and then cut rags for carpet. In evening we were at Klein's for Margret's birthday.

Fri 7 – 29 degrees, warmed up nicely during the day. I patched and we cleaned the brooder house.

Sat 8 – 39 degrees, very cloudy, slow rain for about 2 hours. We took the quilt to Knab's. Another good shower through the night.

Sun 9 – Very cloudy all day. We were at church. Afternoon we visited Mr. & Mrs. Walter Brandenburger. Evening I went to square dance with Metzgers.

Mon 10 – 30 in early morning, fair. I sewed carpet strips.

Tues 11 – 39 degrees. Wachtels picked the bottom corn. Made close to 600 bu in all. Clara was here a while.

Wed 12 – Fair 32 in morning, 69 by noon. We gathered down corn in bottom. Bill & his foreman & son were here hunting. Had supper with us.

Thurs 13 – Fair very pretty day, 40 in morning, 70 by afternoon. We were to Farm Bureau dinner with Roushes.

Fri 14 – Fair 40 in morning, 65 by noon. I washed. Johnny came & had dinner with us. Johnny is working on the Skaer's bridge.

Sat 15 – Fair after heavy fog disappeared, it was foggy till 9:30 a.m. I burned some brush. Then baked pie & coffee cake. Johnny had dinner & supper with us.

Sun 16 – Sunday. We were at church, then stayed home. Went to Hecker card party in evening with Metzgers.

Mon 17 – Fair very warm windy. Johnny was here for dinner. I sewed carpet rags.

Tues 18 – Rained mostly all last night and during the day, clearing by night. Patsy & Mrs. Dennis got me and in evening we went to Bob White Grange for Home Bureau meeting.

Wed 19 – Cloudy cooler. Johnny was here for dinner. Mary & Lillian came in afternoon. I washed & I quilted in evening.

Thurs 20 – 30 degrees fair. I was at Paderborn for Ruth Kreher's wedding. In evening to our guild meeting with Marie Koerber. Quilted during the day.

Fri 21 – Fair 28 in morning, stayed cold all day. I quilted. Evening Metzgers & we were at Bob White Grange card party.

Sat 22 – Fair 30 in morning, warmed up nicely during the day. I baked cookies & quilted. Geo made firewood.

Sun 23 – Very pretty day 54 degrees. We stayed home all day. I finished the quilt. In evening we were at Frank Klein's birthday.

Mon 24 – 45 degrees, started to rain by eleven o'clock & rained all day and all night. I finished planting the tulip bulbs. Mrs. Roush visited here awhile.

Tues 25 – 51 degrees, still raining. Finished hemming the quilt and baked a cake and cleaned up in the house. Went to Grange card party.

Wed 26 – 31 degrees very stormy all night and day. I cleaned the house. Too cold to be outdoors.

Thurs 27 – 20 above. I walked to Schilling's to help cook for the wedding, Ludger's. Nice clear day. Franklin & Gerry & boys came by 2 p.m. Went to Rev. Klem's open house.

Fri 28 – 17 above. Franklin & family & I went to Belleville to take care of business. Also increased our house insurance. Had supper at Bill & Anita's.

Sat 29 – 24 degrees, snowing. Franklin & Gerry & boys left for home at 8 this morning.

Sun 30 – 30 degrees, very cloudy all day. This was Sunday but we stayed home all day.

December 1952

Mon 1 – 30 degrees very cloudy, snow by 2 o'clock while I was at Belleville with Metzgers. Snowed till late in night.

Tues 2 – 30 degrees, very cloudy all day, about 2 inches snow on ground. I ironed & patched.

Wed 3 – 30 degrees, cloudy. Mrs. Roush helped me quilt Patsy's baby quilt. Was very foggy at night.

Thurs 4 – 31 degrees, a lot of the snow melted today. I finished the quilt.

Fri 5 – 30 degrees, fair, very pretty day. I aired the bed things and cleaned all the bedrooms. Geo put tin sheets on brooder house.

Sat 6 – 32 degrees, very pretty day. We cleaned the brooder house yesterday. Today Geo finished the brooder house roof. We were to Mrs. Philip Wirth's funereal.

Sun 7 – 45 degrees, very pretty day. Metzgers got us and we all went to June Ann's birthday party.

Mon 8 – 45 degrees, fair windy. Henry, Edna and Harold were here in the evening.

Tues 9 – 45 degrees warmed up to about 65 to 70. We had the Home Bureau meeting & Xmas party at Mrs. Kemp's.

Wed 10 – Cold northwest winds, cloudy. Geo & I laid the culvert in our road, then the hauler finished hauling rocks on our road.

Thurs 11 – 35 degrees, warmed up to 50 by noon, colder by night. We were at the Grange meeting & Xmas program. I baked cookies.

Fri 12 – 28 in morning, NW winds all day. I baked cookies.

Sat 13 – 22 degrees, snowed off and on during the day. I finished baking Xmas cookies. Johnny was here for supper.

Sun 14 – Cloudy cold all day, 20 in morning, didn't get above 33 all day. It was Sunday, we stayed home. Herman & Melba were here awhile.

Mon 15 – 22 in morning, warmed up to 50 by noon. Mrs. Roush & I were at the Xmas Home Bureau meeting at Hesse's. In evening, officers installed at our Grange.

Tues 16 – 24 in morning, 60 by noon, very pretty day. I washed & ironed.

Wed 17 – Fair very pretty day, 24 in morning, 60 by afternoon. I cleaned the feed house shed.

Thurs 18 – Very cloudy, 36 degrees. I went to Belleville with Roushes to oil meeting. In evening I went to Guild meeting & Xmas party with Metzgers.

Fri 19 – Raining, 40 degrees. I mended socks & worked about the house.

Sat 20 – In morning it was 36 degrees, stayed about the same all day. Evening Metzgers got us and we went to Oscar Koerber's birthday party.

Sun 21 – 33 degrees, cloudy all day. Metzgers & I were to the Robert Philip's funeral. In evening we were at church. Xmas program.

Mon 22 – 37 degrees, light rain all day. I worked about the house. Josephs came in evening and we played cards.

Tues 23 – 37 degrees, cloudy NW winds. I cleaned around the feed house shed.

Wed 24 – Fair not so cold, around 40. I cleaned the house & got half of the turkey at Roush's. Mary & Irv came by 3:30 o'clock.

Thurs 25 – Light snow on the ground. We all opened our gifts. Then had dinner and by 3 o'clock, we all went to Bill & Anita's for supper.

Fri 26 – Much colder 20 degrees. I got a high fever and was so sick I had to stay at Bill & Anita's last night. Today too but felt better after the doctor gave me a shot.

Sat 27 – Cold 20 degrees, light snow. Irwin & Mary & children went to Uncle Henry's then came back to Bill & Anita's and I came home with them.

Sun 28 – Fair warm very pretty day. Viola, Ralph & family were here. Franklin & family came by 6 o'clock evening. So we all had a nice evening together. *Viola Bald is Katie's niece.*

Mon 29 – Cloudy to fair. Irwin went to Denmark farms. Franklin to Belleville. They both came home by suppertime.

Tues 30 – Partly cloudy warm around 45. Mary took me to Dr. Trappe. Afternoon we went to Aunt Edna's, stayed for supper. Franklin & family left for home in the morning.

Wed 31 – 27 degrees, very cloudy all day. Irwin & Mary and children left for home today.

1953

January 1953

Thurs 1 – 34 degrees, cloudy to fair. Pop & I were home alone all day. We spent 2 hours with Josephs to play cards.

Fri 2 – Raining mostly all day, 37 degrees. I washed Johnny's clothes. Snow flurries afternoon.

Sat 3 – 30 degrees. Metzgers got me and we went to our Grange to cook for the conference people. Served 124 dinners.

Sun 4 – 28 degrees, cloudy to fair. Bill, Anita & June were here for dinner. Then I went along to see Elsie Heidenreich at the Red Bud Hospital. Robert Probst's birthday in evening.

Mon 5 – 27 degrees, fair. I washed. It didn't get above 33 all day. Douglas, Millie and son & Mrs. Roush were here in evening.

Tues 6 – 22 degrees, 2 inch snow since last night. I patched.

Wed 7 – 23 degrees & a thin coat of slick ice on ground, lightning thundering by 7 o'clock evening and rained some. Josephs were here, we played cards.

Thurs 8 – 28 degrees still slick outdoors, very cloudy. Raymond drove with their truck and we 3 went to Grange meeting.

Fri 9 – 32 degrees, very slick outdoors, very cloudy & windy by night. We stayed indoors. I patched. Jakie & Cara got wheat for feed.

Sat 10 – 31 degrees, icy all over but melted some, did not get above 32 all day, very cloudy. I sewed carpet strips.

Sun 11 – 27 degrees, fair & windy, NW. Herman & Frank were here for dinner. In evening Metzgers took us along to Walter Etling's. *Herman and Frank Luetzelschwab are Katie's brothers.*

Mon 12 – 31 degrees, fair warmed up to 47. Jakie came got me to go to stay with Johnny. He took me home in evening and took a load of corn home.

Tues 13 – 38 degrees, a beautiful day. We had a nice Home Bureau meeting at Marie Koerber's house. Evening Metzgers & I were at Woodman's picture show. *The Woodmen were a fraternal insurance group with monthly social/business meetings.*

Wed 14 – Around 50 in morning. Joseph and I went to Albert & Elsie's to help butcher. Cloudy all day.

Thurs 15 – Fair 56 degrees, SE winds, very cloudy. We hauled in wood. Afternoon we were at Schilling's. Turned much colder, was 34 by 6 in evening.

Fri 16 – 13 degrees, partly cloudy, stayed cold all day. I washed & ironed.

Sat 17 – 31 degrees, ice on trees and all over, but melted quite a lot by noon.

Sun 18 – 28 degrees, still plenty ice on the ground, melted by evening, fair warm & sunshiney, but muddy. We stayed home all day.

Mon 19 – Cloudy around 32. Johnny came for dinner. Roushes also were here. In evening I was at Klein's quilting while Raymond was at party.

Tues 20 – Very cloudy, 36 degrees, drizzle rain at times. We were at Roush's to see the inauguration of Ike for President on TV. We also dressed 2 ducks.

Wed 21 – Very cloudy foggy. I hurt my leg so I couldn't do much of anything.

Thurs 22 – Very cloudy all day. I went to Clara's for a quilting. In evening we were at Grange meeting.

Fri 23 – Cold rainy all day. I worked in the house all day.

Sat 24 – Very cloudy & strong NW winds. In evening we went to Quirin's with Metzgers.

Sun 25 – Fair 28 degrees. I was at church. Afternoon we stayed home all day.

Mon 26 – 33 degrees, fair very pretty day, warmed up to 64. I dressed 3 hens & brought in wood.

Tues 27 – 32 degrees, fair. I went to Belleville with Alma & Gus. In evening I went to Paderborn card party with them.

Wed 28 – 20 degrees, fair. Geo & I dressed 4 hens for Mrs. Roush. Then Mrs. Roush got me & we dressed their 6 ducks for them.

Thurs 29 – Cloudy & cold, SE wind. Henry finished cutting down the hedge fence. Geo made firewood, I helped.

Fri 30 – Fair to partly cloudy, 42 in morning. I dressed 2 hens. Then cleaned the bedroom. Johnny was here for dinner.

Sat 31 – 47 degrees, fair, very pretty day. I dressed 2 more hens for Roushes. Geo made firewood. Colder by night.

February 1953

Sun 1 – 24 degrees, fair, warmed up to 42 by afternoon. Bill, Anita & June were here.

Mon 2 – Fair beautiful day, 33 degrees. I went to Columbia with Josephs. In evening Metzgers were here. We worked on quilt.

Tues 3 – 31 degrees, got up to 42 partly cloudy. Mrs. Joseph went to the hospital last night. This evening Rapps were here.

Wed 4 – 31 degrees, fair. We cleaned the hen house. Afternoon I went quilting to Marcella's.

Thurs 5 – 34 degrees, cloudy, strong southeast winds. We finished cleaning the hen house. Afternoon our chimney was on fire. Fire department was here.

Fri 6 – 38 degrees. Fair strong NW winds. We cleaned the brooder house & shed. Clara Schilling was here awhile in the afternoon.

Sat 7 – Fair, white frost but warmed up to 55 by noon. I moved things into the brooder house and did my Saturday work.

Sun 8 – 33 degrees, white frost, fair very pretty day. I was at church. Afternoon Edwin Dintelmann, Mrs. Roush and Mr. & Mrs. Leroy Klemm were here. Douglas Roush in evening.

Mon 9 – 46 degrees, fair to cloudy. I washed and made quilt patches.

Tues 10 – 45 degrees, raining slowly at times. Patsy got me and we went to Rapp's for the Home Bureau meeting. Mrs. Roush was here in evening.

Wed 11 – 49 degrees, rained slowly all night. I worked on the quilt patches.

Thurs 12 – Rainy all day. Jakie was here to get wheat. I finished the quilt patches.

Fri 13 – 32 degrees, very cloudy. I went to Millstadt in evening with Metzgers to see the remains of Mrs. Willinberger.

Sat 14 – 26 degrees, fair, very pretty day. I baked cake & rolls. Geo & Raymond cut down part of the willow tree.

Sun 15 – Fair warm, beautiful day. We all went to New Hanover for Lavern & Lucille's wedding. Then stopped at Pearl's & Melvin's a while. *Lavern Lang is Katie's nephew. He married Lucille Ries and they would become 50-year tenants at the Reiss farm from April 1954.*

Mon 16 – Partly cloudy 44 in morning, 32 by noon NW winds. Irv & Mary & children left for home this morning.

Tues 17 – 13 above, fair. Metzgers and I were at Belleville. Then paid our 1951 taxes at Smithton $343.99.

Wed 18 – 36 degrees, fair windy. I washed Johnny's wash and made 2 batches of soap. Sold 100 lbs clover seed to Johnny.

Thurs 19 – 40 degrees, cloudy, rained more thru the night. I was at Tillie Lindaur's quilting today.

Fri 20 – Rained quite hard by afternoon. I was at Schilling's all day to quilt. Got stormy and much colder by night.

Sat 21 – Fair cold 18 above did not warm up over 32 all day. So I mended socks. Johnny was here for supper.

Sun 22 – Fair cold 32 degrees windy. I was at church. Then Bill & Anita & June Ann came. Alma & Gus came & we set up the quilt.

Mon 23 – Fair very pretty day. I baked 2 cakes. Anna Wachtel came & we quilted in afternoon.

Tues 24 – Cloudy 40 degrees. Alma & I had our quilting today. Got it all done, hemmed and all.

Wed 25 – Cloudy 38 in morning. I darned socks. Johnny came afternoon, stayed for supper. Sold my brooder today for $5.00 to Elmer Joseph.

Thurs 26 – 36 degrees, fair & windy. Johnny was here. Brought cherries & strawberries out of his deep freeze for me to cook for him. Grange meeting in evening.

Fri 27 – 38 degrees, warmed up to 52, fair. I washed and cooked strawberry jelly for Johnny.

Sat 28 – 30 degrees, white frost, fair. I did my Saturday work. Mrs. Roush came towards evening.

March 1953

Sun 1 – March came in like a lion, heavy snowstorm all day, down to 25 by evening, then it sleeted.

Mon 2 – 30 degrees, warmed up to 40 and started raining. I sewed quilt patches.

Tues 3 – 35 in morning, 38 by noon, raining quite hard all day, colder by night, thundered during the day.

Wed 4 – 25 in morning, snowing lightly. I sewed on my quilt all day.

Thurs 5 – 30 degrees, fair, warmed up to 50 by noon. Langs sewed clover today. Geo & I went to the Grange to clean & varnish the cabinets & counter.

Fri 6 – 35 degrees, fair to partly cloudy. Johnny was here today. We & Metzgers were at Mrs. Koerber's 90th birthday party.

Sat 7 – Fair in morning, snow by 2 o'clock afternoon, 25 degrees. I baked coffee cake.

Sun 8 – Fair cold 23 degrees. We stayed home all day. Willie & Anita were here a short while. Metzgers took us along to Smithton to see the remains of John Schaub.

Mon 9 – I worked on my quilt. 31 degrees. Then Johnny came and I had to cook jelly for him, also baked pies.

Tues 10 – Cloudy to fair, 35 degrees. Clara & I helped Anna Wachtel quilt. In evening we were at the Home Bureau meeting at Pfennenbecker's.

Wed 11 – Cloudy to fair, 50 in morning, 70 by afternoon. I was at Roush's to sew my quilt lining. Then Geo & I cut down trees to fill gullies.

Thurs 12 – 55 degrees, light rain. Gus, Alma and I were at the Grange to varnish cabinets. Grange meeting in the evening.

Fri 13 – 63 degrees, fair 74 by afternoon. Loretta fixed my hair today. Johnny planted peach trees & apricots. I planted lettuce, beets & carrots.

Sat 14 – 55 degrees, raining to fair, very warm 74 by afternoon, heavy rain by 7 p.m., a lot of thundering. Bill & Anita got their beef at Knab's.

Sun 15 – Fair cold wind all day, nice by night. We had our Grange minstrel tonight. Had a very large crowd. Cleared 260 dollars.

Mon 16 – Jack frost, 35 degrees, fair. Henry & Lavern and Boobie cut down the large trees and burned the hedge.

Tues 17 – 45 degrees, cloudy all day. The men finished burning the hedge. Geo & I went to Arthur Hoffman's quilting in afternoon.

Wed 18 – Fair 40 degrees, northwest wind, rained in the night. I helped Mrs. Joseph quilt all day.

Thurs 19 – 41 degrees, fair. I finished setting a quilt together and also baked rolls. Donald Roush was here. He is back from the Army.

Fri 20 – 40 degrees, fair to cloudy. I spaded a lot in the garden. Also made a new flower bed by feed house, planted onions, carrots, beets & flower seed.

Sat 21 – Fair to cloudy, 47 degrees, very stormy all day. I baked coffee cake. Johnny was here for supper. Geo cut firewood.

Sun 22 – Partly cloudy 50 degrees. I was at church. Edna & Henry were here in afternoon. Had a thundershower then. Edna & I set up a quilt.

Mon 23 – Fair. I washed & ironed and baked a cake for the quilting tomorrow. Around 40 degrees all day.

Tues 24 – Partly cloudy to fair, cold winds all day. 28 degrees. I had 8 ladies in for my quilting. In evening I went to Broad Hollow Grange card party with Metzgers.

Wed 25 – Fair, still cold & windy, 32 degrees. I quilted at Koerber's in the afternoon. Johnny was here for supper. He brought me a cake & ice cream.

Thurs 26 – 28 degrees. I quilted in morning. Afternoon I spaded garden. Grange meeting in evening.

Fri 27 – 31 degrees, stayed cold & windy all day. I finished my quilt then I spaded garden. Johnny was here for supper.

Sat 28 – Fair windy rather cool. I was at the Birkner sale with Metzgers. I planted dahlias and cannas and potatoes in the morning.

Sun 29 – Fair beautiful Palm Sunday. I was at the Smithton church with Metzgers. Kenneth Lindaur was confirmed. Cloudy by night.

Mon 30 – Raining since 6 o'clock a.m., 40 degrees, windy. The Birthday Club was here last night 24 in all. Sylvester Mehrmann was here.

Tues 31 – 56 degrees, raining. I spaded some garden and planted cannas and dahlias.

April 1953

Wed 1 – I baked cookies. Cold & light shower. I cleaned upstairs. Around 46 degrees during the day.

Thurs 2 – I cleaned the house. Irwin, Mary & children came by 8:45 p.m.

Fri 3 – Fair cool 47 windy. Irwin, Mary & Kenny went to the south farms. Bill, Anita, June and Johnny were here for supper.

Sat 4 – 35 degrees, fair, warmed up to 60 by noon. We all went to Bill & Anita's afternoon & stayed for supper.

Sun 5 – Easter Sunday, very cloudy, 39 degrees. We all went to church. Started to rain slowly by noon. Bill, Anita & June came for dinner. Franklin & family came by 5 p.m.

Mon 6 – 40 degrees, cloudy to fair. Franklin & family left for home by 9:30 a.m. Irwin & family left for home by10:30 a.m. I went to Mrs. Schilling's for a short while.

Tues 7 – 36 degrees, fair. We voted today. Then I washed and patched some. I gave to agent $3.00 for Country Gentleman renewal.

Wed 8 – 50 degrees, very hard rain by 8 o'clock a.m. I was to Marie's quilting. Rained with some hail by 8 p.m.

Thurs 9 – Fair very warm or hot, 55 in morning to 89 by afternoon, turning colder by night. Geo & I were to the Grange meeting in evening.

Fri 10 – Fair cold wind all day, 42 to 55 degrees. Metzgers took us along to Broad Hollow Grange for the degree work.

Sat 11 – 44 degrees, fair to cloudy, rain by afternoon and into night. I did my Saturday work. Josephs sawed their wood today.

Sun 12 – 40 degrees, very cloudy, stayed cold all day. This was a lonesome Sunday, nobody came and we didn't go anywhere.

Mon 13 – 38 degrees, fair, very pretty day. I was at Roush's to sew together quilt blocks. It warmed up to 56 by afternoon.

Tues 14 – Fair cool. Patsy & Mrs. Dennis got me and we went to the Home Bureau meeting at Mrs. Elmer Probst's. We had an apron sale, made $9.75.

Wed 15 – Cloudy & very stormy getting colder. Alma & I quilted at Mrs. Arthur Hoffman's. Wind was so strong one could hardly walk outdoors.

Thurs 16 – 33 degrees, fair to cloudy. I sewed on a quilt. Marie Koerber took me along to the Guild meeting.

Fri 17 – 40 degrees, very cloudy, rain by afternoon & colder, 33 by 9 p.m. Jakie brought all the bricks for our new cistern. *Jacob Luetzelschwab is Katie's brother. The new cistern is to be dug on the north side of the newer Reiss house built in 1941 and collect rainwater from the roof.*

Sat 18 – 28 degrees, snowing heavy about an inch at six a.m., about 4 in by 10 a.m. Willie & family came and we all went to Sikeston for the weekend.

Sun 19 – 28 degrees, cloudy to fair & cold all day, light snow flurries they told us. We were to Uncle John's. It was sunshiney then. Got home by 6:30 then went to the Grange.

Mon 20 – Still cold NW winds but fair, 32 degrees at midnight when we came back from the Grange birthday program & party.

Tues 21 – 45 degrees, fair. We were at the Paderborn card party. Mrs. Dennis, Mrs. Glauber & I were at the funeral home to see Mrs. Scholes.

Wed 22 – Fair. I worked about the place. Geo celebrated today by reading & resting.

Thurs 23 – 56 degrees, fair to cloudy by night & rained hard by 8 p.m. We celebrated Geo's birthday at the Grange meeting.

Fri 24 – Fair & warmer. We had a very hard rain last night. Anita got us for June Ann's play. We stayed overnight.

Sat 25 – 50 degrees, fair very stormy. We planted flower seed & tomatoes at Bill & Anita's. Then we went to Lang's for supper, Harold's & Delores's wedding reception. *Harold Lang is Katie's nephew. He married Delores Schuchardt.*

Sun 26 – Rainy all day, 40 degrees. Carlena & Elmer and Christie and Herman & Frankie were here for dinner. Elsie & Albert & Harvey came in the evening.

Mon 27 – 40 degrees, later 62. I washed & then spaded garden, planted peas. Geo chopped down old peach trees.

Tues 28 – Fair to cloudy & windy, 57 in the early morning. I spaded garden & planted sweet corn & pickles, also peas & tomatoes & cabbage seed.

Wed 29 – 60 degrees, very cloudy. I planted more sweet corn & cucumbers also sugar melon. Rained hard by night, very windy all day.

Thurs 30 – 61 degrees, too wet to work outdoors, so I baked 2 cakes and coffee cake. Had company several times. Light thundershower. Got up to 75 degrees.

May 1953

Fri 1 – 69 degrees at 6 a.m., 80 by afternoon, very windy, turned to west. I was in Belleville with Metzgers. Then I planted more cucumbers & a few watermelons.

Sat 2 – Fair, very pretty day. I prepared for Sunday dinner. Mr. & Mrs. Walter Brandenburger visited with us in the evening.

Sun 3 – 50 degrees, very pretty day. The Hesse & Heidenreich families & Bill, Anita and June Ann had dinner with us. We celebrated Bill's birthday.

Mon 4 – 46 degrees, very cloudy all day. We brought wood in and I mixed feed and marked the quilt.

Tues 5 – Raining so I set up Mrs. Knab's quilt & quilted a lot. Mrs. Joseph helped.

Wed 6 – 51 degrees. I spaded some and planted more potatoes also flower seed. Rain hard by evening. Mrs. Joseph helped me quilt.

Thurs 7 – 54 degrees, partly cloudy. I went to Hecker church guild doings in afternoon, then I spaded some.

Fri 8 – 52 degrees very pretty day. I worked in the garden all day, planted flower seeds, cucumbers and sweet corn.

Sat 9 – Fair very pretty day, got up to 80, but cool again at night. Josephs planted corn out by orchard. I planted more cucumbers & watermelons.

Sun 10 – 64 degrees, Mother's Day. We went to church. Afternoon Ed & Lottie came also Mr. & Mrs. Mike Mueth and Bill, Anita & June came towards evening.

Mon 11 – 61 degrees, got up to 80 by noon, partly cloudy to fair. I hoed my garden. Johnny came towards evening. We went along to look at the things he wants to sell.

Tues 12 – 65 degrees, cloudy. I prepared for the Home Bureau meeting. Jakie brought out the vanity & kitchen cupboard, also other things. 16 members were here & also 10 children.

Wed 13 – Rainy 50 degrees, getting cooler. I quilted mostly all day. Pomona meeting at night.

Thurs 14 – 40 degrees, rainy in morning, cloudy all day. Johnny got me & we cleaned his house. Tillie & Edna also helped. Grange meeting in evening.

Fri 15 – 54 degrees, cloudy to fair. I spaded in the garden, planted more sweet corn & watermelons.

Sat 16 – 59 degrees, rained hard during the night and all morning till about 3 p.m. I quilted most all day.

Sun 17 – 60 degrees, partly cloudy, rain as church let out. Got a hard rain and storm by 3 p.m., nice by 6. Schillings were here in the evening.

Mon 18 – Fair by afternoon. I washed. Mrs. Birkner & Mrs. Gasser came afternoon and we started to piece the contest quilt.

Tues 19 – 65 degrees, fair. Mrs. Hoffman got me & Mrs. Kirleis and we went to the annual Home Bureau meeting at Belleville at Elka's.

Wed 20 – 52 degrees. I went to Mike Mueth's to cook for Celestine's wedding, very pretty day, also went along to Smithton in evening.

Thurs 21 – 70 degrees, got up to 85. I mowed lawn & pulled weeds. Went to Guild meeting in evening.

Fri 22 – 73 degrees, very cloudy, windy to fair. I prepared things, baked. Mary, Irv & children came at 9:30 p.m.

Sat 23 – 67 degrees, partly cloudy, hard rain by afternoon while we were at Uncle Henry's. We all had supper at Bill & Anita's.

Sun 24 – 68 degrees, fair. Irv, Mary and children & Pop & I went to the Reiss Reunion at Earl & Helen's house. Irv & Mary went home that evening. *Earl Reiss is George's first cousin once removed. He and Helen hosted cousins' reunions for 50 years.*

Mon 25 – 72 degrees in morning, got up to 93 by afternoon. I worked about the house. Ed & Lena Becker were here last night.

Tues 26 – 77 degrees in morning, got up to 97 by afternoon. I was at Belleville with Metzgers. In morning I hoed garden.

Wed 27 – 60 degrees, very pretty day. I washed & ironed. Spaded garden and afternoon Johnny got us & we went to Louis Keim's to celebrate Mrs. Hoffman's 90th birthday.

Thurs 28 – 63 degrees, windy, fair. I spaded garden & hoed a lot of weeds out. We were at Grange meeting. I was ladies assistant steward.

Fri 29 – 62 degrees but got quite warm by noon 87. I spaded more & chopped weeds. Also I ironed.

Sat 30 – 73 degrees, got up to 89. I hoed garden & Geo made wood in morning. We were at Roush's and Knab's in afternoon.

Sun 31 – 72 degrees. We were at church. Afternoon Alma & I went to Veda Chaffin's shower. Evening we were to Alma's birthday party.

June 1953

Mon 1 – 73 degrees. Johnny & Jakie came to start on the cistern.

Tues 2 – 56 degrees, fair. Henry & Lavern Lang helped ½ day with the cistern. Raymond helped in the afternoon.

Wed 3 – 52 degrees, fair, got warm today. Johnny, Jakie and Geo & I worked on the cistern.

Thurs 4 – 62 degrees, windy. Langs, Jakie & Johnny all worked on our cistern. All dug and started to lay bricks.

Fri 5 – 74 degrees at 6:30 a.m. Langs, Jakie & Johnny bricked the cistern today.

Sat 6 – I washed for Johnny & us and ironed a big wash for Roushes & cut some weeds. Bill, Anita & June were here in evening.

Sun 7 – Fair around 90 by noon. We had our strawberry social & cold supper at the Grange.

Mon 8 – Hot winds all day, 95 by afternoon. Johnny & Jakie made the concrete slab for the cistern top.

Tues 9 – Fair hot 97 to 100 by afternoon. Alma & I cooked for the Rapp's wedding.

Wed 10 – Hot around 98. I rested today. Johnny was here for supper. In evening I paid Wachtel $32.25 for fertilizer.

Thurs 11 – Very hot sultry 92 at noon, then a cool wind for Mrs. Roush. Josephs combined barley. We were at Grange meeting.

Fri 12 – 99 degrees. I finished ironing and patched some.

Sat 13 – 72 in early morning, got up to around 100 by noon. We picked our first dewberries. I baked a cake. Light shower by night.

Sun 14 – Cooler 72 in morning, 85 by noon, very cool in evening again. Johnny took us to Sister Mary's birthday. We all enjoyed the day.

Mon 15 – 68 degrees. Geo & I picked 2 gal dewberries. Lang's, Jakie & Johnny came and plastered the cistern & laid the slab on top.

Tues 16 – 79 in early morning, 93 by noon, windy from SW. Johnny & Jakie finished the spouting for cistern. I went to H.B. meeting at Mrs. Dennis'.

Wed 17 – I was at the Schaefer wedding. Henry Langs came in evening.

Thurs 18 – 75 degrees in morning, 103 by afternoon. I picked 6 qt dewberries & we put them in the deep freeze.

Fri 19 – Hot winds 105 degrees. We picked 3 qts dewberries. Then dressed 5 chickens at Roush's. Langs were here in evening.

Sat 20 – Hot winds 105 by 4:30. I washed in the morning & we cleaned the granary. Bill, Anita & June were here in evening.

Sun 21 – 73 in morning, 97 by 3:30 p.m. I baked 2 cakes & helped Langs unload 1 load of wheat. Herman & Frank came in afternoon.

Mon 22 – 63 degrees at 6 a.m., 97 by afternoon. Langs finished combining.

Tues 23 – 70 degrees at 6 a.m., got up to 92. Mary, Irv & children came by 6 p.m.

Wed 24 – Around 98 by afternoon. Mary & Irv left to go to some meetings. They stayed at Bill & Anita's overnight.

Thurs 25 – Around 100 by afternoon. I finished the Grange pillow cases. Mary & Irv came back by 7 p.m. Then Geo & I went to the Grange meeting.

Fri 26 – Nice & cool after a hard rain through the night. Irwin went to the south farms.

Sat 27 – 97 by noon. Irv, Geo & I were at Waterloo & bought a stove combination electric. Hesses, Bill, Anita & June were here in evening.

Sun 28 – Partly cloudy thundered by afternoon, very little rain, 87 degrees. Irv, Mary & children left for home at eleven in the morning.

Mon 29 – 85 during the day. I washed. Afternoon the Schneider's men brought the combination stove & set it up.

Tues 30 – 95 by noon. I ironed and worked about the house.

July 1953

Wed 1 – Very hot all day. I picked cherries. Then went to Belleville with Metzgers. In evening Johnny took us along to Pearl & Melvin's.

Thurs 2 – 81 in early morning, got up to 96 by afternoon. I canned cherries & dug some potatoes.

Fri 3 – 81 in early morning, got up to 90, partly cloudy. I finished canning cherries, got 11 quarts. I saw a few corn tassels out today.

Sat 4 – 70 degrees, 85 by noon, rained slowly from 10:30 to 12 a.m. Johnny cut down the bed head end. I cleaned the porch.

Sun 5 – 82 in morning, 92 by 11 a.m. I was in church. Then we slept. Got up to 101 by 4 p.m. at six we walked to Schilling's.

Mon 6 – 79 in early morning, 82 by noon & cooler towards evening. I washed & cleaned upstairs.

Tues 7 – 80 in morning, 93 by afternoon. I patched and pulled weeds. We picked 3 quarts blackberries.

Wed 8 – 71 degrees in morning, warmed up to 86. Ed & Lena spent the afternoon with us, they took apples along.

Thurs 9 – 61 degrees, stayed cool & fair all day. I baked cake & pie and worked about the house & yard. Grange meeting in evening.

Fri 10 – 63 in the morning, 82 by noon. Franklin, Gerry, George & Richard came at 5 p.m.

Sat 11 – 61 degrees in morning, got up to 85 by noon. We all were at Millstadt in morning. Franklin went to Highland in afternoon.

Sun 12 – 62 in morning, got up to 89. We all were at church. Bill, Anita & June came & we had dinner. Went to Turner picnic to eat fish in evening.

Mon 13 – 65 degrees, got up to 87 by afternoon. Franklin & family left at 5 a.m. to go to Texas. I worked about the house & cleaned up.

Tues 14 – 67 degrees in morning, 92 by afternoon. I cut weeds under apple trees, then canned apple sauce. Home Bureau meeting at Mrs. Barthel's in evening.

Wed 15 – 65 in early morning, had a light rain in the night. I got apples and canned them, also washed & ironed.

Thurs 16 – 71 degrees, got up to 92. Canned apples again and did the patching.

Fri 17 – 78 degrees, got up to 95, thundered but no rain. Geo & I brought in more apples and canned them. Johnny worked on the water system.

Sat 18 – 70 degrees in morning, got to 96. Bill & Johnny set up our water system. Pop & I went to Paderborn picnic. I washed dishes for Lena Klein.

Sun 19 – 75 in morning, 95 by afternoon. Geo & I dug up the sewer in morning, then slept awhile.

Mon 20 – 76 in morning, 96 by noon. Geo & I worked on sewer again, then I worked in the house. Henry Lang finished plowing the 8 acres.

Tues 21 – I helped set up the contest quilt at 8 a.m. & quilted till 10 a.m. Then Frank, Gerry, the boys & I went to Belleville. Went quilting again in the evening. Rained at night.

Wed 22 – 72 in morning, 90 by noon. We finished the contest quilt at the Grange. Franklin took a picture of it. Were at Viola's for supper.

Thurs 23 – 62 in early morning. The children went to Bill & Anita's and St. Louis. I washed & ironed. We were at the Grange meeting.

Fri 24 – Getting hot. We baked peach & apple pies. Went to the lake for a wiener roast supper. Had fun feeding grasshoppers to the fish.

Sat 25 – 78 at 6 a.m., 102 by 4 p.m. I canned apples also gathered more apples. We all went to see the parade at Smithton. Ate fish for supper.

Sun 26 – 102 by afternoon. We all went to church at Belleville. Ate dinner at Bismarks. Went to show, Ma & Pa Kettle. Jacob Leiner and Robert Ehret paid $20 for hunting on Schaefer ground.

Mon 27 – 75 in morning, 102 by 3 p.m. Franklin, Gerry, Geo & Richard left at 7 a.m. for home. Then I washed and worked about the house. Johnny came for supper.

Tues 28 – Still hot 102 by afternoon. I worked with the apples, also ironed.

Wed 29 – 79 at 7 a.m., 105 by 4 p.m. We could only work in early morning, then tried to keep cool in the living room.

Thurs 30 – 80 degrees at 6 a.m., 104 by 4 p.m. I cooked apple preserves and canned apples & beans. Johnny was here for supper.

Fri 31 – 85 degrees at 6 a.m. I picked up a bu of apples. Then washed Johnny's clothes. Lavern & Lucille were here in the evening. Rained light shower.

August 1953

Sat 1 – 80 degrees in early morning, 100 by 4 p.m. I canned 5 quarts of apple sauce.

Sun 2 – 79 in early morning, 100 by late afternoon. We were at church then we ate dinner at Woodmen picnic. Went home to rest. Then went to picnic again with Metzgers for the evening.

Mon 3 – 80 by 6 a.m. I chopped weeds, then picked up apples, then peeled apples to can.

Tues 4 – 79 degrees, got up to 87 by afternoon, light shower. We chopped weeds all day. Sold the last June apples today, 2 bu to Gassers.

Wed 5 – 70 in morning, got up to about 90, but very cool by evening. We & Metzgers were at the fair. Johnny was here for supper.

Thurs 6 – 62 degrees at 6 a.m., 87 later. I chopped weeds, then dug some in the sewer. Also washed.

Fri 7 – 62 degrees in morning, 88 by afternoon, light shower towards evening. We & Metzgers were at the Broad Hollow Grange meeting.

Sat 8 – 62 in morning, stayed cool all day, a shower by 5 p.m. We pulled weeds in the chicken yard, also made some firewood.

Sun 9 – 57 degrees, fair. We were at church. Church meeting in the afternoon. In evening Bill, Anita and June Ann came.

Mon 10 – 62 degrees. Sister Mary & Lillian came and stayed overnight. We canned peaches and darned socks.

Tues 11 – 63 degrees, warmed up to 94. We potted house plants also the violets only a few plants in all. Mary & Lillian went home today.

Wed 12 – 72 in morning, we had a good rain in the morning, clearing by noon. I pulled weeds, also canned some peaches. Johnny was here for supper. Paid our Monroe Co. taxes which were $10.28.

Thurs 13 – 72 degrees, 90 by noon. I canned peaches also baked cake. Were at the Grange meeting in evening.

Fri 14 – 70 degrees. I canned peaches and worked about the house. Franklin, Gerry, Geo & Richard came at 8:30 in evening.

Sat 15 – 68 degrees. We all went to Belleville. Then to Bill & Anita's, then to St. Louis Hospital to see Bertha. Had supper at Bill & Anita's. Stopped at Lang's.

Sun 16 – 72 degrees, got up to 85, cloudy. Bill, Anita & June came also Johnny. Franklin & family left for home by 2 p.m.

Mon 17 – 70 degrees, 90 by noon. I canned peaches. Geo worked along the road by the mailbox.

Tues 18 – 63 degrees, got up to 85. I washed. Also picked peaches and put some in the deep freeze. Cooked tomato preserves.

Wed 19 – 53 degrees. I was along to the Home Bureau meeting at Bob White Grange.

Thurs 20 – 57 degrees. I canned peaches & worked about the house. Was to the Guild meeting with Metzgers.

Fri 21 – 58 degrees, warmed up to 95. I dressed Robert Schneider's chickens. Irv & Mary and the children came by 7 in evening.

Sat 22 – 65 in morning. Mary, Irv and Ken & Mary Kay went to Denmark farm. I fried chicken for the Grange supper. Stevie stayed here and went to picnic with us.

Sun 23 – 65 in morning, 96 by noon. Edgar & Toddy & children were here in morning. Bill & Anita came and had dinner with us all. Went boat riding (*probably at the Sportsmen's Lake*).

Mon 24 – 70 in morning, 98 by 4 p.m. Irv & Mary and the children left for home at 10 o'clock. We didn't do much. Helped clean at the Grange in evening.

Tues 25 – 63 in early morning, 102 by 4 p.m. I washed & canned peaches. Geo worked by the road cleaning brush.

Wed 26 – 63 at 6 a.m. I worked about the house and got things ready to go to Urbana. We got one load of Raw Rock on rye pasture.

Thurs 27 – Cool 64 at 3 a.m. when we left for Urbana, got there at 7 a.m. We had a nice day with watching ball games.

Fri 28 – We and Koerbers were at Urbana overnight with Gerry and the boys. Franklin was on a trip. Came home at 9:30 p.m.

Sat 29 – 65 at 6 a.m., 98 by noon. I washed a few things and worked about the house. Schillings were here in evening.

Sun 30 – 70 in morning, 102 by afternoon.

Mon 31 – 70 at 6 a.m., 104 by 4 p.m. We were at Roush's to peel peaches and tomatoes for canning. We were at the Woodmen outing yesterday.

September 1953

Tues 1 – 65 in morning, 104 afternoon. We paid our Millstadt taxes $1.84. Then I cooked tomato preserves.

Wed 2 – Around 70 in morning, 101 by afternoon. I started to chop brush by the mailbox.

Thurs 3 – 69 in morning, 100 by noon. Geo & I chopped hedge & brush at the mailbox. Afternoon we rested. Very cloudy afternoon. Got our oil lease check from Texas $160.00.

Fri 4 – Good slow rain towards morning and much cooler, 57 at 7:30 a.m., stayed cool all day. We chopped trees & brush again.

Sat 5 – Fair cool 58 in morning, stayed cool all day. Johnny was here for dinner. We & Metzgers went to the Millstadt Homecoming in evening.

Sun 6 – 60 degrees, warmed up to 85. Metzgers took us along to the Waterloo Homecoming.

Mon 7 – 50 degrees, stayed cool all day. We chopped brush in morning, then I washed. Albert Hoffman's were here in evening.

Tues 8 – 49 degrees, got up to 80. We chopped wood by the road. I went to Belleville with Elmer Kabureck on account wheat acreage.

Wed 9 – 50 degrees, 82 by noon. We made firewood and went to Bluff Grange for Pomona meeting & contest. We got 3rd on our quilt.

Thurs 10 – 64 degrees in morning, 90 by afternoon. I canned cling stone peaches & visited with Schillings. Grange meeting in evening.

Fri 11 – Hot winds all day, got up to 97, cooled off at night and was cool on Saturday.

Sat 12 – 65 degrees, stayed cool all day. We got milk at Roush's then I cleaned upstairs.

Sun 13 – 44 degrees, stayed cool all day. We went to church. Then Bill & Anita & June and Johnny came and had dinner with us.

Mon 14 – 65 degrees, got up to 80. We chopped brush along the road in morning. Bill & Anita took us along to Sportsman's Fair yesterday.

Tues 15 – 46 degrees in morning, 80 by noon. We cleaned brush along the roadside, then I sewed carpet strips & worked about the house.

Wed 16 – Josephs picked some corn today. Alma & I helped Ida & Irene Gasser to clean the Grange Hall.

Thurs 17 – 58 degrees, got up to 96 by noon. Alma & I were at Ida Gasser's to help prepare for the wedding supper for Irene & Melvin. Were along to church.

Fri 18 – 69 degrees, 100 by noon, hot winds all day. I worked about the house. Geo stayed indoors all day.

Sat 19 – 65 degrees, 95 by noon, light rain last night.

Sun 20 – 60 degrees. We were at church, was up to 90 by noon. Bill & Anita & June were here to work on the hot water system.

Mon 21 – 50 degrees, stayed cool all day. I washed & ironed and was at the District Home Bureau meeting at Broad Hollow Grange with Loretta Probst.

Tues 22 – 40 degrees at 7 a.m., 65 by noon, 70 by 3 p.m. We chopped brush along the road.

Wed 23 – 50 degrees, got up to about 80. We cleaned the hen house this morning, then I started to clean up the brooder house.

Thurs 24 – 58 degrees, got up to 80. I potted flowers and cleaned up around the house. We went to the Grange meeting with Metzgers.

Fri 25 – 60 degrees, got up to 80. I potted flowers and brought them on the sun porch. Went to Broad Hollow Grange in evening with Koerbers.

Sat 26 – 55 degrees. I worked in the basement.

Sun 27 – 60 degrees. I went to church afternoon. Metzgers took us along to visit Mrs. Dara Mueth & family.

Mon 28 – 62 in morning, 98 afternoon. Worked in woods by the mailbox. Afternoon I worked in the basement.

Tues 29 – 66 degrees, hot winds all day. I went to Belleville with Metzgers. In evening we all went to Booster Night.

Wed 30 – 62 in morning, 91 by noon. I worked by the mailbox, then I washed.

October 1953

Thurs 1 – 55 degrees at 6 a.m., got up to 80 by noon. Johnny took us to Waterloo, then Anita called for us to come & go to hospital to see Henry.

Fri 2 – About 60, 89 by noon. We stayed with Bill & Anita all night & today. Went to see the football game and saw June lead the band, then we went home.

Sat 3 – 62 degrees, hot by noon. Louis & Hattie came by afternoon & stayed till Monday. Took us along to visit Earl & Helen on Sunday. *Louis Reiss is George's brother from Texas.*

Sun 4 – Henry passed away at 5 a.m. Rained all day today. Louis & Hattie went to Centralia to get clothes to go to Henry's funeral on Wednesday. *Henry Reiss died today at age 73 in St. Louis.*

Mon 5 – Fair & cool today. I potted more flowers. Mueths got us in evening & we went to Broadview Hotel in East St. Louis to Grange conference.

Tues 6 – 37 degrees. Louis & Hattie came & we all went to St. Louis to funeral home to see Henry. Irv & Mary & children came in evening.

Wed 7 – 40 degrees, fair very pretty day. We all went to Uncle Henry's funeral, then visited with Bill & Anita awhile. Josephs finished sowing wheat.

Thurs 8 – 42 degrees, fair. Irv & Mary and the children left for home. We were at Grange meeting in evening.

Fri 9 – 50 degrees. I baked & cleaned the house. Franklin, Gerry & boys came by 9 p.m. Henry Lang will finish sowing wheat tomorrow.

Sat 10 – 60 degrees. Johnny & Jakie came & laid the tile in our sewer. Afternoon Franklin, Gerry, the boys and I went to visit Aunt Bertha.

Sun 11 – 62 degrees. We all went to the lake & got pears in morning. Bill, Anita & June came. Franklin & family left for home by 1:30 p.m. We were at Mrs. Klein's birthday in evening.

Mon 12 – 60 degrees, cool all day. I worked about the house. Canned tomato pulp. Mrs. Roush was here awhile.

Tues 13 – 48 degrees, stayed cool all day. I was at Smithton with Mrs. Roush. Alvina Rapp took me to the Home Bureau meeting at Ida Gasser's in evening.

Wed 14 – 42 on front porch. I washed & ironed. Helped clean Grange Hall for card party.

Thurs 15 – 50 degrees. I baked pies for women's Guild meeting in the evening. Marie came & got me.

Fri 16 – 50 degrees, got up to 80. We made some firewood. In evening we were at Broad Hollow Grange for program exchange.

Sat 17 – 60 degrees, got up to 85. Johnny took the awnings off and puttied & painted 8 windows. I also cleaned in the brooder house.

Sun 18 – 48 degrees, warmed up to 92. We were at church. The Brinkers came for short visit. Then we & Metzgers went to Progressive Grange Wurstmarkt.

Mon 19 – 50 degrees, warmed up to 90. I painted the north rain cap of sun porch.

Tues 20 – 55 degrees, warmed up to 89 by noon. We had our Grange card party. Cleared $166.

Wed 21 – 60 degrees. Johnny & Jakie were here. Finished the sewer and then puttied & painted windows. I also painted some.

Thurs 22 – 63 degrees. I baked pies & painted the lawn bench & chair. L. E. Williams brought the last of lumber. I paid him $242.94 for 4,049 feet @ $60.00.

Fri 23 – 62 degrees, cloudy NW winds, getting cooler. Geo & I were at Roush's and then we piled up some lumber. I also washed.

Sat 24 – 42 degrees, fair cool all day. Katie Petry came at noon to stay till Sunday evening.

Sun 25 – 34 degrees, stayed cold all day but fair. Mr. & Mrs. Ed Cook & Mable Reiss were here also Johnny. Katie left with the Cooks. We were at church.

Mon 26 – 43 degrees & cloudy, started to rain slowly at 10:30 a.m., rained all day and night.

Tues 27 – 51 degrees, some light rain and getting colder. We went to card party with Oscar Koerbers to Paderborn.

Wed 28 – 42 degrees, partly cloudy. Wachtels brought us our third corn. We put it in the barn, made about 200 bu for our share.

Thurs 29 – 33 degrees white frost. We stacked some lumber. Ed Feders were here for dinner. In evening we went to see Edgar Jennings at funeral home. *Ed Feder is George's first cousin on his mother's side.*

Fri 30 – 35 degrees, white frost. We piled lumber.

Sat 31 – 38 degrees. We piled lumber mostly all day. Johnny was here for a while.

November 1953

Sun 1 – 40 degrees. Alma & Gus got us to go to church, then from there we went to Woodland Grange dinner wurstmarkt. Walter Etling came in evening.

Mon 2 – 46 degrees, very foggy & wet. I picked apples then finished stacking lumber.

Tues 3 – 50 degrees, cool all day. We visited with Mrs. Anna Wachtel, then we gathered walnuts, then I cleaned the car shed.

Wed 4 – 33 degrees, cold NE winds. I worked in the house in morning. Afternoon I raked some of the outside yard.

Thurs 5 – 28 degrees, white frost. We worked about the house and yard. Johnny was here a while.

Fri 6 – We worked about the place. Johnny came at 3 p.m. We then all went to Pearl & Melvin's for Dale's second birthday.

Sat 7 – 26 degrees. I baked 2 cakes and canned apple sauce and did my Saturday work. Geo made firewood.

Sun 8 – 24 degrees. Johnny and Mr. & Mrs. Beaber & son and Bill, Anita & June were here for dinner. We were to Gus Metzger's birthday in evening.

Mon 9 – 25 degrees. I washed and patched and brought in some apples. Mrs. Roush was here awhile.

Tues 10 – 30 degrees, white frost. I ironed and raked lawn and picked apples & hauled in firewood.

Wed 11 – 28 degrees. I raked the lawn & burned leaves. Then I worked in the house. Canned apple sauce.

Thurs 12 – 28 degrees, heavy white frost. Geo & I walked to Roush's to go to Farm Bureau meeting & dinner with them. Grange meeting in evening.

Fri 13 – 30 degrees, very pretty day. Jakie, Johnny & Joseph put a new roof on granary shed. Geo & I cleaned up some of old hen house by the grove. *The granary is a log building built in 1834 by Adam Reiss who founded the family farm that year with an initial purchase of 120 acres.*

Sat 14 – 35 degrees, very pretty day, warmed up to 73 by noon. I planted rose hips. Loretta Dohrman fixed my hair, a Tonie. Bill & Anita came for supper.

Sun 15 – 40 degrees, 72 by noon. Langs took us along to Vera's, it was her birthday in evening. We stayed at Lang's. Metzgers also came.

Mon 16 – 40 degrees, very pretty day, got up to 73 by noon. I painted, also Jakie painted. Johnny & Jakie put posts under granary shed and cut and set yard light pole by feed house.

Tues 17 – 42 degrees. I painted on the house. Afternoon I went to Home Bureau meeting at Mrs. Wm. Schneider's. To 4H card party in evening.

Wed 18 – 53 degrees, partly cloudy. I painted a while. We were to the Broad Hollow Grange card party with Mueths.

Thurs 19 – 54 degrees, south winds. I painted a while, then went to Schilling's. Marie & I were to Guild meeting in evening.

Fri 20 – 61 degrees in morning, light showers, clearing by noon. Johnny was here for dinner, then I went to Belleville with Metzgers. Filled out farm papers.

Sat 21 – 35 degrees, windy from SW. I painted a while. Romauld Schilling fixed up our yard light.

Sun 22 – 40 degrees, raining lightly, clearing by noon. We stayed home all day. Went to Frank Klein's birthday party in the evening with Metzgers.

Mon 23 – Fair cold 38. I cooked a kettle of soap. Went to visit Marcella in afternoon. Joseph told us today that he will move soon.

Tues 24 – 48 degrees, windy. I washed & ironed. Cut out the soap & brought it in.

Wed 25 – 36 degrees, cloudy light snow flurries getting colder, very stormy from northwest. I worked about the house. Franklin & family came in evening.

Thurs 26 – 32 degrees. We all went to John Reiss's at Sikeston for Thanksgiving Day. Got there at about one o'clock noon, had a very nice time with Lonnie & Lillian. *Lillian Standley is John Reiss's daughter. John Reiss founded the Reiss Dairy in 1926 and brought his son-in-law Lonnie Standley into the business in 1935. For many years they printed poems written by Sikeston customers on their glass milk bottles which are now highly collectable.*

Fri 27 – Around 30 degrees, fair. We all had dinner with Lonnie & Lillian, then everybody left for home. Irwin & Franklin & Bill and family all spent the evening here.

Sat 28 – 24 degrees, fair. Franklin, Gerry and the boys left for home this morning. Mary & Irv took us along to their home today.

Sun 29 – Around 28 degrees. Irv & Mary and the children went to Sunday School & church while Pop & I rested. Mary & Irv left for Chicago in afternoon.

Mon 30 – Cold & windy. Pop & I took care of the children. Mary & Irv will come home on Tuesday evening.

December 1953

Tues 1 – Mary & Irv came home at 8 o'clock this evening.

Wed 2 – Fair & warmer to cloudy. Mary did the washing then we went shopping. Irv went to Indianapolis.

Thurs 3 – Rained slowly. Afternoon Irwin took us along to the Clinton Farms. We also went down to the coal mines.

Fri 4 – Colder to fair. Mary and I went Christmas shopping. Irv worked at the office. Children were at school.

Sat 5 – Warm, got up to 52. We all worked about the yard, rain by night.

Sun 6 – Colder very cloudy and windy. The children all went to Sunday School. Afternoon Mary & Irv went to Bloomington.

Mon 7 – 40 degrees, very pretty day. Irwin took us home today, got here at about 3 o'clock. At 4 o'clock Irv left for the Denmark Farm.

Tues 8 – 40 degrees, fair cloudy and rain by midnight. I was at Mrs. Roush's study party in evening.

Wed 9 – 37 degrees, warmed up to 60 but getting much colder by afternoon. I was at Belleville with Metzgers.

Thurs 10 – 24 degrees, warmed up to 50. Metzgers took us to the Grange meeting. We celebrated Mike Mueth's silver wedding anniversary.

Fri 11 – 30 degrees, cloudy all day. I started cleaning upstairs. Johnny came for dinner.

Sat 12 – 34 degrees, fair very pretty day. Geo & I walked to Roush's to get meat. Then I cleaned upstairs.

Sun 13 – 32 degrees, cloudy all day. Herman & Frankie were here for dinner. Schillings were here in afternoon.

Mon 14 – 24 in morning with snow flurries, strong NW winds got down to 20 by midnight. I washed. In evening we and Metzgers were at Grange for degree work for 4 Granges.

Tues 15 – 20 degrees, warmed up to 40, fair. We had around 250 people at our Grange last night. Progressive & Prosperity Granges put on 1st & 2nd degrees.

Wed 16 – 17 above, a few snow flakes, strong NW winds. Johnny & Lavern came and started on ceiling our upstairs. Was cold all day.

Thurs 17 – 7 above, clear did not get above 21 all day. Lavern & Johnny worked on the upstairs again. I was at Guild Xmas party with Metzgers in evening.

Fri 18 – 15 above, getting warmer, cloudy. I baked some cookies.

Sat 19 – 30 in morning, got up to 38. I washed for Mrs. Roush. We & Metzgers were at Turkey Hill Grange to see the 3rd & 4th degree work.

Sun 20 – 35 to 45. Josephs moved today. I baked cookies. Johnny was here for dinner. Were at church Xmas program in evening.

Mon 21 – 40 degrees, cloudy all day. Alvina & Doris got me and we went to Mrs. Grieble's Home Bureau Xmas party.

Tues 22 – 6 above, stayed cold all day. We were at Grange Xmas party. Pop stayed home. He had a cold.

Wed 23 – 4 above, fair got up to 20 by noon. I baked & prepared things for Xmas.

Thurs 24 – 13 above, warmed up to 42. Metzgers & I were to the little Ross boy's funeral at Smithton. Irv, Mary & children came in evening.

Fri 25 – 24 degrees, getting warmer. Franklin & family and Bill & family & Irv & family all had supper with us.

Sat 26 – 40 degrees, very pretty day. Afternoon Irwin, Pop, Johnny and the children & I went to the Lake to skate. Men worked in the hall.

Sun 27 – 34 degrees. Franklin & Gerry and the boys went home on Saturday morning. We all were at St. Louis to see Bertha this morning. Were at Bill & Anita's for dinner.

Mon 28 – 32 degrees, fair. Mary & Irwin and the children went home this morning. We gave Josephs the release today. We had officers' installation at our Grange.

Tues 29 – 25 degrees, heavy jack frost. I washed, then Johnny came and we gathered 4 sacks of corn on Schaefer's place. Warmed up to 45 by noon.

Wed 30 – 30 degrees, very cloudy. I ironed & cleaned up about the house.

Thurs 31 – 24 degrees, warmed up to about 40 by noon. Lucille & Lavern came & hauled some wood in for us. Geo made firewood.

Epilogue: 2008

Quilting, grange, church, farming, family, and friends combined very well for Katie and George Reiss. She lived to age 96 and he to age 91. But now all their siblings, those spouses, and their three sons have passed on to a greater reward. The Reiss Family Farm continues with ownership in the fourth and fifth generations such that we will celebrate 175 years of its existence with a family reunion on June 6, 2009. Katie's and George's DNA and legacy live on through 6 grandchildren, 11 great grandchildren, 5 great great grandchildren, and a great great great grandchild.

Katie's Diary effectively provides a five-year window into life on the Reiss Family Farm.

www.ingramcontent.com/pod-product-compliance
Lightning Source LLC
Chambersburg PA
CBHW061353280526
45784CB00001B/241